10

DATE DUE

JAN 0 5 2015		
JAN 1 5 2015		
FEB 5 2015		
FEB 2 6 2015		
APR 2 2015		

THAT'S NO ANGRY MOB, THAT'S MY MOM

THAT'S NO ANGRY MOB, THAT'S MY MOM

TEAM OBAMA'S ASSAULT ON TEA-PARTY, TALK-RADIO AMERICANS

MICHAEL GRAHAM

Since 1947
REGNERY
PUBLISHING, INC.
An Eagle Publishing Company • Washington, DC

Cataloging-in-Publication data on file with the Library of Congress

ISBN 978-1-59698-619-0

Published in the United States by
Regnery Publishing, Inc.
One Massachusetts Avenue, NW
Washington, DC 20001
www.regnery.com

Manufactured in the United States of America

10 9 8 7 6 5 4 3 2

Books are available in quantity for promotional or premium use. Write to Director of Special Sales, Regnery Publishing, Inc., One Massachusetts Avenue NW, Washington, DC 20001, for information on discounts and terms or call (202) 216-0600.

Distributed to the trade by:
Perseus Distribution
387 Park Avenue South
New York, NY 10016

This book is dedicated to the millions of Americans who showed up at tea parties and townhalls across America during the Revolution of '09. The politicians never knew what hit 'em.

In fact, they still don't. That's why I wrote this book.

Table of Contents

Chapter One

My Mother, the Terrorist

Meet Patricia Graham—wife, grandmother, office manager, churchgoer, community volunteer. And in her spare time, rightwing domestic terrorist.

She's also, depending on who's doing the talking, an "evil-monger," a "white supremacist," a "hater," a "tea-bagging redneck," a "dangerous mutation," and part of an "angry mob."

And she's my mom.

How did this mild-mannered woman from Columbia, South Carolina, go from "happy homemaker" to "hate-mongering radical?" That's the funny part—she hardly did anything. To paraphrase Woody Allen, 90 percent of being labeled a rightwing lunatic is just showing up—especially at a tea party. That mundane action can get the gentlest American denounced on the cover of national magazines, condemned by White House officials, and outted on MSNBC as an agent in the vast rightwing conspiracy to overthrow our government and declare a NEW FASCIST ORDER!

Pretty impressive for a woman who usually can't find her own car keys.

I love my mom, and she's a woman of many talents. But somebody, somewhere, is getting carried away. Setting aside her superhuman ability to torture me, my sister, and my dad, the word that best describes my mom is "normal." She works forty-plus hours a week. She pays her bills and her taxes. She keeps an eye on her neighbors' house when they're out of town, and she volunteers with local community groups. She makes a meatloaf that will turn a cowboy into a vegan in one sitting. And she has a feather boa and matching high heels I once stumbled upon in her closet, whose purpose is too disturbing to contemplate.

Overall, she's a typical, proud, patriotic, law-abiding prototype of a mature American woman, one who cries watching life insurance commercials while wearing a Snuggie and sitting in her favorite chair. If I were auditioning terror-inspiring radicals, she wouldn't get a callback.

And it's not just my mom who's being misrepresented. Look at the tea party attendees in your hometown or in thousands of communities across America. These aren't masked anarchists smashing windows and setting fires at a G-20 summit. They aren't angry, "Bush Lied, People Died" sixties throwbacks using a political rally to score some pot from their grandkids' classmates.

Sure, there are some oddballs at tea parties. And the Obamabesot media will get every kook photographed, quoted, and featured on the front page of the biggest newspapers. But the tea party and townhall gatherings are oddly, almost bizarrely... ordinary. They comprise retirees, military vets, small business owners, and suburban families. Byron York of the *Washington Examiner*, for example, was at the huge Washington, D.C., tea party on September 12, 2009. He reported,

> No one I met expressed hatred for the president. A few had voted for him, and others, like Christy Smith, said they were deeply moved when he was elected. Many others opposed him all along. But now, the predominant mood is deep distrust. They believe Obama will raise their taxes, that he will blow up the health care system, that he will weaken America's defenses.... You've probably heard descriptions of the marchers as crazies and haters and fanatics. Perhaps there were some in the crowd. Far more important, though, was the very presence of so many everyday Americans protesting in Washington.
>
> What did Barack Obama and his party's leadership on Capitol Hill do to bring doctors and truck drivers together in common cause on the streets of the nation's capital? More than anything, these people are afraid that the new president is running the country off a cliff.

So hundreds of thousands of Americans congregated on the Washington Mall, chanted some slogans, listened to speeches criticizing excessive government spending, and then went home without incident. And what did they get for their trouble? They were denounced as racists, threats to our democracy, and would-be Lee Harvey Oswalds.

Why have these painfully polite, terribly typical people—folks who look less like bomb throwers and more like the early-bird special crowd at a Denny's in Branson, Missouri—come under constant assault from the elite media, the Washington establishment, and the Obama administration? What makes my mom such a threat?

Like I said—she's normal. And in Barack Obama's America, "normal" is the new "freak."

America: Obama's Little Green Acre

In the Obama era, normal "bitter, clingy" Americans—you're probably one of them—are under assault. The Obama elites are engaged in a coordinated campaign of character assassination designed to redefine your values into venalities and to transform traditional American character strengths into shameful flaws.

You don't want to pay higher taxes, and you think hard work should be rewarded? You're unpatriotic.

You don't understand how the solution to a disastrous economy caused by massive debts, spending, and bailouts is to add trillions in new debts, spending, and bailouts? That's because you're dumb.

You don't like your tax dollars being used to reward scammers who bought $500,000 homes on $55 incomes? You're unfair, heartless, and—of course—racist.

Always racist. Or some variation, like "bigoted" or "hateful." This has been the Left's reaction to tea partiers since the movement first began. On April 16, 2009, one day after the movement took full force with hundreds of tea parties staged nationwide, leftwing activist Janeane Garofalo went on Keith Olbermann's *Countdown* to explain what the movement was really about. Having seen masses of Americans turn out on Tax Day to protest the government's fiscal irresponsibility, Garofalo drew a strange conclusion: "This is about hating a black man in the White House," she proclaimed. "This is racism straight-up. That is nothing but a bunch of tea-bagging rednecks."

The accusation of racism is now the alpha and omega of American politics. Loyal O-bots—those fawning, unthinking followers of the president—play the race card in every discussion and every debate. Obama's Senate consigliore, Harry Reid, even compared opponents of the Democrats' healthcare "reform" to defenders of slavery. So if you ladies don't want a nanny government agency deciding if you can have a mammogram, you might as well put the hood back on, because Harry Reid has figured you out.

Stupid, backward, bigoted, racist. You've probably been called all this and more, all by people who simultaneously decry partisanship and divisiveness. And if you're like my mom, then you kept quiet for a while. You're not a political activist. You're not a talk show host or TV bigmouth. You're just a normal American. You're just a citizen, a taxpayer, a parent.

Then one day, you had enough. You got tired of the attacks on private enterprise. Or maybe you didn't like seeing the government saddle your children and grandchildren with unsustainable debts. Or perhaps you just got sick of the Obama-era theme that being American means always having to say you're sorry, that you should be ashamed for just being you.

So you finally did something. It was probably something small like writing your congressman, calling in to a talk show, or slapping a bumper sticker on your cubicle wall asking, "How's that hope and change working for you?" And that's when it happened. That's when you found out just how big this fight is, and that you are in it. That's the day you became a "hater."

Then you went to a tea party, and that's when you really crossed the line. Every morning the newspaper calls you a dangerous, hate-filled kook. Every night, the TV news declares you an ignorant, potentially violent redneck. And in between, political pundits and even politicians denounce you with juvenile

Love Letter from the Left

"This was the closest thing to a mob that I've ever experienced in my life."

—Democratic senator Max Baucus, on tea party protestors

insults like "teabagger." Taxpayer-funded National Public Radio even graced its website with an animated attack on the movement titled, "Learn to Speak Tea Bag."

Because they're so much smarter than you, of course.

It's an endless barrage that has average Americans asserting that maybe it's "time to take our country back"—only to be told that liberals have declared this phrase a hate crime.

The nonstop attacks even have everyday people questioning their own sanity. At least, that's what happened to my mom. "I'm watching these people on TV claiming we're going to spend a trillion dollars and it won't cost us anything and that the government is going to fix my healthcare, when I know the government messes up just about everything," she told me. "They say anyone who disagrees is hateful, and I wonder if they've gone crazy, or if it's me."

No, Mom, it's not you. It's them. *They* are insane. The lefty loonies, the mind-numbed Obama worshippers, the snarling media goons, the campus kooks, the frightened seekers of PC approval—they've all gone nuts. But they've done it in the same way and at the same time, which makes us normal people wonder if it's the Left that's crazy or if it's us.

You know what it reminds me of? That hilarious 1960s TV sitcom, *Green Acres*. The main character, Oliver Douglas, is a rational, level-headed farmer in Hooterville, a town where everyone else is crazy. In every episode, Oliver's neighbors posit some ridiculous theory—say, that Mr. Ziffel's "son" Arnold (he's actually a pig) needs to get a driver's license—and Oliver laughs it off. Undaunted by reason or logic, the Hooterville crowd (no relation to the well-endowed waitresses at your local wing joint) press on. And because they share the same brand of insanity, their craziness is defined as normal.

Of course, the nuttiness of Hooterville is a fantasy. In the real world, pigs don't get drafted into the army. Chickens can't lay square eggs. And the government would never pay farmers hundreds of thousands of dollars *not* to grow... uh, never mind.

Anyway, in *Green Acres*, the rational, normal guy is always right. But because everyone around him is insane in the same way, *he* looks like the kook. Even Oliver's ditzy wife (played by then-hottie Eva Gabor—yeah, baby!) gets pulled into the lunatic loop by sheer force of numbers.

Inevitably, the last scene of each episode would show Arnold the pig driving away in a convertible as Oliver looks on in astonishment. Insanity had seemingly become reality.

But that was only a sitcom. This is America: Barack Obama's Little Green Acre.

Rise of the Rabble Rousers

The Obama elites often claim the tea party movement is a centrally-run, corporate-controlled, well-funded enterprise. After all, that's the only way *they* can get anything done. So they dismissed the initial townhall protests against Obama's healthcare takeover as a stage-managed Astrotuf campaign. Chris Matthews ridiculed the protestors as "well-dressed, middle-class people in pinks and limes."

"The last time I saw well-dressed people doing this was when Al Gore asked me to go down to Florida," sniffed Senator Barbara Boxer, invoking the Democrats' ridiculous victim complex stemming from the 2000 elections. "I was confronted with the same type of people."

Well, I've got bad news for these folks who attribute the tea party movement to a vast, well-organized plot: the very first tea partier had to ask the Seattle Parks Department where to hold her conspiracy.

"Oh, yeah," laughed Keli Carender when I asked her about the story. "I knew the first thing I had to do was pick a location. I started with Seattle police, they put me in touch with the Parks Department to get a permit. When I talked to the guy, I told him, 'I don't even know where to hold an event like this,' and he told me, 'Most of the protesters use this one park.' So I said, 'Okay.'"

And that February phone call started it all. Thirty-year-old Keli had decided to do something, and now she knew where to do it. She was motivated by her opposition to Obama's extravagant $787 billion stimulus bill—or "Porkulus" as she called it. Keli had called her congressman and senators to complain, but their voicemails were jammed. "So I decided either I could stay home and feel depressed or I could go out and do something even if it didn't make a difference. I knew it would make me feel better, and maybe other people would feel better, too."

And so, on President's Day 2009, some 120 people showed up in downtown Seattle at the first Obama-era tea party—all because a young lady who teaches basic math to inner city adults took it upon herself to give her fellow citizens a space to speak out.

Three days later, on February 19, from the floor of Chicago's futures exchange, CNBC correspondent Rick Santelli unleashed his "rant that launched a thousand protests"—and counting. Rick didn't know Keli Carender, but he could have been reading her mind when he ripped into the Obama administration for "promoting bad behavior" by bailing out delinquent mortgage holders:

Rick Santelli: I'll tell you what, I have an idea. You know, the new administration's big on computers and technology—how about this, President and new administration? Why don't you put up a website to have people vote on the Internet as a referendum to see if we really want to subsidize the losers' mortgages; or would we like to at least buy cars and buy houses in foreclosure and give them to people that might have a chance to actually prosper down the road, and reward people that could carry the water instead of drink the water?

Trader on Floor: That's a novel idea.

(applause and cheering)

Joe Kernen: Hey, Rick? Oh, boy. They're like putty in your hands. Did you hear...

Santelli: No they're not, Joe. They're not like putty in our hands. This is America! How many of you people want to pay for your neighbor's mortgage that has an extra bathroom and can't pay their bills? Raise their hand.

(traders booing)

President Obama, are you listening?

...We're thinking of having a Chicago tea party in July. All you capitalists that want to show up to Lake Michigan—I'm gonna start organizing.

(whistling and cheering)

...

Wilbur Ross: Rick, I congratulate you on your new incarnation as a revolutionary leader.

Santelli: Somebody needs one. I'll tell you what, if you read our founding fathers, people like Benjamin Franklin and Jefferson—what we're doing in this country now is making them roll over in their graves.

That night Michael Patrick Leahy, who had founded "Top Conservatives on Twitter" (#TCOT) as a place for conservatives and small-government activists to share ideas, received several voicemails from people who were fired up by Santelli's rant. According to Leahy,

> I'd been involved in enough grassroots efforts to know that [Santelli's proposed tea party] was too far away. We had momentum right then. So we held a conference call with other activists the day after Santelli's rant and decided we needed a "Nationwide Chicago Tea Party" right away.
>
> One group already had an event planned for February 27, so I asked [fellow activist] Eric Odom to hold one in Chicago at the same time. Then we worked from there, trying to get as many people in as many places to just hold an event— whatever size—so we could have multiple protests across the country.

Influential bloggers like Michelle Malkin and Instapundit's Glenn Reynolds got behind the idea, resulting in the staging of fifty tea parties around February 27 with some 30,000 attendees, all organized in a week.

"Immediately people started talking about another event, so we decided April 15—Tax Day—was the way to go," Leahy told me. "We started a website: nationwidechicagoteaparty.com. The website name was long and clumsy, but people seemed immediately to get the idea."

The April 15 rallies were much bigger than anyone expected—more than a million people attended some 900 tea parties across the country. This marked the real emergence of the tea party movement. And instead of quickly fizzling out like many liberals expected, the movement has only grown—to the point that a hypothetical tea party candidate polled better than a generic Republican in a December 2009 Rasmussen survey. Among independent voters, the tea partier was more popular than either a Republican or a Democrat.

For folks on the Left who rely on unions and so-called "walkin' around money" to motivate people, the notion of true grassroots action like this is hard to grasp. Dana Loesch, a blogger and radio talk host in St. Louis, explained how it works.

"A friend of mine who's been involved in protests called me while I was on the air one night and said, 'We've got to organize an event under the Arch, it's got to be big, and we've got to do it in two days!' It sounded like a good way to get into trouble, so I said, 'Sure!'"

Two days later, on February 27, they were part of the first tea party wave. It turned out, Dana's listeners weren't mind-numbed robots waiting for orders. They were already looking for a way to get involved, too. They just wanted her to give them the time and place.

"People who listen to talk radio and attend townhalls are genuinely interested in what's going on in our country," Dana told me. "They're not necessarily from one party or another. One of our first tea party protestors was a guy who campaigned for Barack Obama. He still had the bumper sticker on his car. It's sad that we've turned a fundamental belief like limited government into a partisan issue."

Ned Ryun, son of GOP Congressman Jim Ryun, was another early tea partier. When organizers of an April 15 tea party in

Richmond, Virginia, approached him about speaking, he didn't expect much of a turnout. "But when I got there, we had 5,000 people crammed in this little park. It was forty degrees and raining. You just don't see that kind of passion very often. It was a great experience."

Ned confirms what all of us who organized tea party or town-hall events experienced: "It was completely spontaneous, organic." Leahy told me the people at his tea party were "the kind you'd find at a PTA meeting. Lots of independents, lots of disaffected Republicans who didn't like all the spending under the Bush administration."

And I had the same experience. My radio station hosted the Boston Harbor Tax Day Tea Party at the urging of local listeners who had been inspired by the February tea parties. They were enthusiastic, but they clearly had no experience organizing anything. If a corporate Astroturf organization had been handy, I would have happily handed the event over to them.

But thanks to some great local folks, we had a tremendous turnout on the Harbor. We tossed our tea chests into the sea and added our voices to the million more across the nation.

Unsurprisingly, the Massachusetts "newspaper of record," the *Boston Globe* (or the *Boston Globe-Democrat*, as it's known on my show), refused to cover the protest. It was actually comical. Just days before the Tax Day tea parties, the *Washington Post*'s Howard Kurtz reported that the *Globe* hadn't run a single story about the tea party movement. Boston is, after all, the birthplace of the "tea party" concept. Really, isn't that deserving of at least *one* story?

It got worse. I picked up the *Boston Globe* on April 16—the day after thousands of BOSTON-area citizens gathered at BOSTON Harbor for a BOSTON tea party...and found one tiny story. It was a small item from the AP wire services, buried on page A16.

It began, "Dateline— Frankfort, KY."

If there's a conspiracy, it's not from the townhall and tea party crowd. These Americans aren't part of any Astroturf, SuperMob, or vast conspiracy of any kind. They're just regular people who've figured out you can't trust what you hear from Washington, and you can't trust what you read in the papers. And they're people who think it's time somebody did something about it.

People like Keli Carender of Seattle, Washington, and Pat Graham of Columbia, South Carolina.

> ## Love Letter from the Left
>
> "Dad, you're the most dangerous thing on the political landscape because you're a sixty-year-old white conservative, and that's more terrifying than any jihadist."
>
> —Hollywood director Joe Carnahan, maker of *Narc* and *Smokin' Aces,* to his father

Our future: The United States of Amherst?

I joined the tea party movement because I don't like the direction Obama is taking this country. And I know exactly what that direction is. Because I've been to Amherst.

A small town in western Massachusetts, Amherst is mostly known as the home of the University of Massachusetts' main campus. And it's the home of some of America's most insanely liberal politics.

Coincidence? Or something more . . .

It's a town entirely dominated by America-loathing O-bots. Think I exaggerate? After a UMass professor testified that our flag is "a symbol of terrorism and death and fear and destruction and repression,"an Amherst town meeting rejected a proposal to formally fly the American flag more frequently. Another meeting participant called the flag "intimidating" and "a symbol of militarism." The date of that vote? September 10, 2001. And the massacre of nearly 3,000 Americans the following day wasn't enough to change their minds. In fact, Amherst has rejected multiple proposals to fly the U.S. flag on September 11 to commemorate the loss of American life that day.

One of the leading opponents of these proposals was liberal activist and future O-bot Ruth F. Hooke.

During the Bush administration, Hooke supported resolutions calling for the impeachment of President Bush and Vice President Cheney; the immediate withdrawal of all troops from Iraq; and granting non-citizens the right to vote in local elections. She earned widespread attention in 2009 when she proposed that freed Guantanamo detainees be relocated to Amherst. "There has been a lot of fear-mongering all around the country," Hooke said, adding she wanted to "help change the popular view. . . . These [cleared detainees] are not hostile people."

One Amherst board member who backed Hooke's Gitmo plan said she voted yes after realizing her fear of the detainees had been "propagandized" into her. Another "yes" vote said the detainees deserved to come to America since they were "suffering because of the U.S. government." Hooke added, "They sound like fine guys. They'd fit right in Amherst."

Truer words . . .

And the people of Amherst apparently agreed, because their town meeting representatives voted to welcome any and all freed "victims" of Guantanamo Bay.

There's a *Green Acres* moment for you—Gitmo detainees are encouraged to wander around town, just as long as they're safe from the offensive sight of an American flag. I bet if you told Khalid Sheik Mohammed about Amherst, he'd ask, "Where did you find those extremist whackjobs?"

Typical Americans look at the people of Amherst—and Cambridge, Manhattan, San Francisco, etc.—and we understand that our values are going to be in the minority in those communities. That's part of their quaint, if clueless, charm.

Out in normal America, we just laugh when we hear about oddball liberal towns trying to criminalize smoking in private homes, or declaring themselves nuclear-free zones, or banning "unauthorized chasing games" (a.k.a. tag) at their public schools. We ask ourselves, "What will those loonies think of next?"

But it's beginning to dawn on more and more typical Americans that, in the era of Obama, *we* are becoming the oddballs. If you don't want Gitmo detainees in your town, or you oppose granting civil rights to foreign terrorists, or even if you just fly the American flag, then someone's likely to ask you, "What the hell is wrong with you? What are you, some kind of weirdo?"

You certainly will be, in Team Obama's "United States of Amherst."

So, will liberal insanity become America's new normal? Will you end up being as out of place in Main Street, America, as you would be in Berkeley or Cambridge?

It's tough to say. Obama's election stemmed from several factors coming together in 2008: a talented, charismatic Democratic candidate running against an uninspiring Republican; the sincere desire of Americans to elect a black president; the political ineptitude of the George W. Bush administration and the arrogance of Washington Republicans; the economic meltdown; and the liberal activism of the mainstream media. As a result, America is witnessing a unique political moment, and it's hard to predict whether things will keep moving in this direction or if we'll reverse course.

But one thing's for sure: the politicians who govern us right now have almost nothing in common with their people. All of those kooky ideas you used to snicker at in college, all those campus nuts who wouldn't shut up about how smart they were, but who knew nothing about the real world—they're the ones in charge.

The challenge is for typical Americans like my mom to "cling" desperately to our fundamental values of personal responsibility, economic opportunity, and common sense. These used to be the shared ideals among nearly all Americans. But in Obama's America, they're considered symptoms of political dementia.

There's nothing wrong with you, Mom. They're wrong, and you're right. So right, in fact, that instead of answering your concerns about bailouts, stimulus spending, and healthcare, they just attack you.

You're right: presidents are supposed to love and celebrate America's exceptional place in the world.

You're right: congressmen are supposed to work for the American people, not attack our character and bury our children under an avalanche of debt.

You're right: people are supposed to be responsible for their own bills, their own debts, and their own families.

You're right: the free market, not the government, creates jobs.

You're right: grown-ups want a government that treats us like adults, not like overgrown children waiting for some government bureaucrat to take our temperatures and wipe our noses.

You're right: the world is still a dangerous place, and our enemies cannot be hugged into submission.

You're right about all these fundamental American values, even if our government, our media, and our elites mock you and demean you.

So tell 'em to go screw.

You're right, they're wrong. And even though you feel outnumbered, you're really not. Sure, the Obama elites dominate the media, academia, and Hollywood. But according to a Gallup poll released in October 2009, among the American people overall, conservatives outnumber liberals by a stunning 2 to 1 margin.

Can we stand up for common sense? Can my mom help defend our national character from this assault by the Obama elites? Can everyday Americans rescue our country from this moment of insanity?

We tea partiers know the answer: yes, we can.

Chapter Two

Right-Wing Terrorist A-Holes of America, Unite!

It was just another day in Obama's paradise.

One morning at the height of the ObamaCare debate, I got an email from my friend Jonah Goldberg at *National Review Online* asking, "Have you seen this?" There was a link to a website urging supporters of government-run healthcare to turn September 11, 2009, into a "call your senator" day. Here's how the website read in part:

> All 50 States are coordinating in this—as we fight back against our own Right-Wing Domestic Terrorists who are subverting the American Democratic Process, whipped to a frenzy by

their FOX Propaganda Network ceaselessly re-seizing power
for their treacherous leaders.

...DEFEAT ANTI-DEMOCRATIC FORCES OF HATE
WHO CONSPIRE TO REMAIN HEALTHY + WEALTHY
WHILE THE PUBLIC LANGUISHES UNDER THE BUR-
DEN OF OUR PRESENT HEALTH CARE SYSTEM

Further down the page was this exhortation:

RECLAIM OUR LAND FROM THE HEIRS OF, YES: BIN
LADEN. YOU KNOW IT'S TRUE.

Opponents of a controversial healthcare proposal are "rightwing
domestic terrorists?" They're *the heirs of Bin Laden?* What nut
job website is this from? MoveOn.org? The *Huffington Post*?
IStillTakeMichaelMooreSeriously.net?

No. It was posted at *www.BarackObama.com.* Yes, *that* Barack
Obama. It was the official website of his presidential campaign.

I read the page several times in disbelief. Then, not an hour
later, I got another email. Sent by a listener, it can be paraphrased
in this family-friendly book as follows: "Holy cow, I can't believe
my [flaming] eyes. What did this [very bad person] call us?"

He attached another web link, which led to a video of a public lecture by a prominent liberal activist in early 2009. It showed
an audience member complaining that Democrats can't get as
much done with their large majority in Congress as Republicans
did with smaller ones. "Why can Republicans push things
through and we can't?" she asks.

"The answer to that is, they're a**holes," the speaker replies.
On videotape. In front of a big, liberal crowd. Without apology.

Once again, who would throw around the "A" word in a public speech? Bill Maher? A renegade Dixie Chick?

No, it was Van Jones—a former Communist, self-described "black nationalist," and supporter of convicted cop killer Mumia Abu Jamal. Oh, and for much of 2009, he was a key member of the "post-partisan" Obama administration. He'd probably still be working for Obama today, only bloggers uncovered the fact that Jones signed a public statement demanding an investigation of the Bush administration's supposed conspiracy to allow the September 11 attacks to happen.

What a day. I'd been called a terrorist, a force for hate, and an a**hole—all by representatives of the Obama White House—and it wasn't even lunchtime yet.

I know there's plenty of name-calling in politics. In fact, I support it. One of the mottos of my radio show is, "If you can't say something nice—call me!" Pithy, on-point labels help us quickly identify the lunatics among us—labels like "Birther," "Truther," and "Dan Rather."

And as a talk radio host and writer, I get called names all the time. No complaints—it comes with the job. I'm used to it. But these comments weren't just aimed at me. As a bona fide tea partier, my mom was also a target.

She and other townhall-attending, Glenn Beck-watching Americans are apparently now terrorists. And it's not just the Obama website that says so—the accusation also comes from the arm of the Obama administration that's in the business of arresting, shooting, and killing actual terrorists. Don't believe me? Read this passage from a report by the Department of Homeland Security, conveniently released to local law enforcement just as the tea party movement was taking off in April 2009:

> The DHS/Office of Intelligence and Analysis (I&A) has no specific information that domestic rightwing terrorists are currently planning acts of violence, but rightwing extremists

> may be gaining new recruits by playing on their fears about several emergent issues. The economic downturn and the election of the first African American president present unique drivers for rightwing radicalization and recruitment.

And who are these "domestic rightwing terrorists?" The report states, "Rightwing extremism in the United States can be broadly divided into those groups, movements, and adherents that are primarily hate-oriented (based on hatred of particular religious, racial or ethnic groups), and those that are mainly antigovernment, rejecting federal authority in favor of state or local authority, or rejecting government authority entirely."

So if you're "antigovernment," you need to be watched as a potential terrorist threat? Then DHS better round up everyone stuck in line at the DMV. Talk about a hotbed of potential antigovernment terrorism; two hours of trying to get a government moron to register your car could turn a mild-mannered librarian into a bomb-throwing anarchist.

Now read the very next sentence of the DHS report: "[Rightwing extremism] may include groups and individuals that are dedicated to a single issue, such as opposition to abortion or immigration."

Being pro-life makes you a possible domestic terrorist? If so, then forget Osama bin Laden—what are we going to do about the *Pope*? I don't know about you, but until all the Catholic bishops are cooling their frocks in Guantanamo Bay, I'll be sleeping with one eye open.

If opposing abortion is "extremism," then at least 51 percent of Americans are extremists, according to Gallup. And if opposing illegal immigration makes one a radical, then America is a nation of radicals. According to an October 2009 CNN poll, a whopping 73 percent of Americans want the number of illegal immigrants decreased—the highest percentage to date.

The DHS report also includes this observation: "Rightwing extremist chatter on the Internet continues to focus on the economy, the perceived loss of U.S. jobs in the manufacturing and construction sectors, and home foreclosures."

The economy, job losses, and home foreclosures? Apparently "rightwing chatter" means you're reading the business section of the *New York Times*.

Americans who care about issues like illegal immigration, federalism, big government, or unemployment—these aren't terrorists, extremists, or kooks. In fact, they're probably a majority of the voting public. But that hasn't stopped the Obama elites from using the "extremist" label to malign these Americans in the national media. As Jesse Walker observes in *Reason* magazine, the vague language of the DHS report serves to marginalize mainstream conservative groups by lumping them in with the extremists. And as Walker notes, the DHS report was hardly a one-off fluke:

> Government-run "fusion centers" in several states have produced similar papers aimed at identifying "potential trends or patterns of terrorist or criminal operations"; the subjects range from anarchists to Odinists to "Illicit Use of Digital Music Players." The most infamous dossier, produced by the Missouri Information Analysis Center, was devoted to the remnants of—what else?—the militia movement, plus a host of other dissidents it roped in with the militiamen. The fact sheet, which was distributed to police throughout the state, declared that "it is not uncommon for militia members to display Constitution Party, Campaign for Liberty, or Libertarian material. These members are usually supporters of

former Presidential Candidate: Ron Paul, Chuck Baldwin, and Bob Barr."

Why of course—it's all so clear now! "Ron Paul '08" bumper sticker = rightwing extremist = militia member = loading the fertilizer and diesel fuel into the pick-up and heading to the nearest federal building. Why didn't I see that before?

This full-blown (pardon the pun) attempt by the Obama administration and its allies to tar typical Americans like my mom with the "terrorism" brush is an outrage. It's also ironic, given these same liberals go apoplectic whenever anyone uses the t-word to describe Muslims marching through London shouting "Death to the Infidels!" Perhaps this has escaped Ms. Napolitano's notice, but nobody's getting their shoes x-rayed or their underwear examined at airport security due to tea party violence.

The profiles of the 1993 World Trade Center bombers, the 9/11 hijackers, the shoe bomber, the Fort Hood jihadist, and the would-be Jockstrap Bomber of Flight 253 all have something in common—and it's not their opposition to government spending. I'll give you a hint: it begins with "I" and ends with "slam." But even if the Obama administration doesn't notice that, we can all thank our president for keeping us safe from the terrible specter of "rightwing terrorism."

Call her the "Grassy Knoll Grandma"

Of course, it's not only the Obama administration that demonizes tea partiers as violent lunatics. Leftwing activist groups are leading the charge, and their false accusations reverberate in the echo chamber of the mainstream media. You almost have to admire these groups' rhetorical skills: since there has been no actual violence associated with tea partiers, they rely on hysterical warnings about the ever-present *threat* of violence. Just take a look at this jeremiad from the self-declared "liberal media watchdog," Media Matters for America:

> A President was killed the last time right-wing hatred ran wild like this.
>
> That being John F. Kennedy, who was gunned down in Dallas, of course.
>
> I've been thinking a lot of Kennedy and Dallas as I've watched the increasingly violent rhetorical attacks on Obama be unfurled. As Americans yank their kids of [sic] class in order to save them from being exposed to the President of the United States who only wanted to urge them to excel in the classroom. And as unvarnished hate and name-calling passed for health care "debate" this summer.
>
> The radical right, aided by a GOP Noise Machine that positively dwarfs what existed in 1963, has turned demonizing Obama—making him into a vile object of disgust—into a crusade. It's a demented national jihad, the likes of which this country has not seen in modern times.
>
> But I've been thinking about Dallas in 1963 because I've been recalling the history and how that city stood as an outpost for the radical right, which never tried to hide its contempt for the New England Democrat.
>
> . . . [T]he truth is, America's most famous bouts of political violence (i.e. JFK, Oklahoma City, etc.) have always been accompanied by waves of radical, right-wing rhetoric. Given that history, the GOP's insistence that the hate now filling the streets couldn't possibly inspire violence seems woefully naive.

So my mother seems to be part of a violent movement threatening the very existence of our republic. She has, after all, waved a sign at a tea party rally. And I can personally testify that she is indeed dangerous—especially when she has to parallel park.

As for the allegations that she and her fellow tea partiers are linked to the JFK assassination, however, I happen to know that in November 1963, my mother was in Los Angeles tending her precious newborn son, a handsome and precocious infant who would one day grow up to become a conservative heartthrob—desired by women, admired by men, and feared by...

Huh—what? Am I still typing?

Sorry, I got a little distracted there. The point is, connecting the Kennedy assassination to tea parties nearly half a century later is a pretty ridiculous stretch. In fact, I can absolutely guarantee that we'll never see another "rightwing" assassin like Lee Harvey Oswald. Not because there isn't some nut out there who wants to assassinate the president; but because Lee Harvey Oswald was...a *Marxist*.

This is hardly news to anyone who's watched more than thirty minutes of the History Channel. When the folks at Media Matters and many other lefties try to link tea partiers to the "rightwing violence" of 1963, they have to distort Oswald's actual politics. As Jonah Goldberg wrote in *Liberal Fascism*,

> The fact that Oswald was a communist quickly changed from an inconvenience to proof of something even more sinister. How, liberals asked, could a card-carrying Marxist murder a liberal titan on the side of social progress? The fact that Kennedy was a raging anticommunist seemed not to register, perhaps because liberals had convinced themselves, in the wake of the McCarthy era, that the real threat to liberty must

always come from the right.... Never mind that Oswald had already tried to murder the former army major general and prominent right-wing spokesman Edwin Walker or that, as the Warren Commission would later report, Oswald "had an extreme dislike of the rightwing."

But the accusation persists today. In 2009, *New York Times* columnist Bob Herbert wrote a column about the "garbage" and "racism" that supposedly characterized the opposition to President Obama's policies. He concluded that liberals should "think about the Oklahoma City bombing, and the assassinations of King and the Kennedys. On Nov. 22, 1963, as they were preparing to fly to Dallas, a hotbed of political insanity, President Kennedy said to Mrs. Kennedy: 'We're heading into nut country today.'"

Today, liberals like Mr. Herbert consider the entire nation—with the possible exceptions of Manhattan and San Francisco—"nut country." And he repeats the JFK slur, and throws in Bobby's murder for good measure. Given that Bobby Kennedy was assassinated by Sirhan Sirhan, Herbert apparently blames that crime on the Vast Rightwing Conspiracy, Palestine Division.

Now, there are kooks in any big movement, and that includes the tea party movement. Undoubtedly, when you have thousands of people at a tea party rally, you're going to have a few "Obama: Muslim Agent of Kenyan Commies!" signs to balance out the "Haliburton Hurricane Machines Caused Katrina!" banners you find at leftwing protests. But the attempts by the Obama elites to link concerned conservative citizens to Sirhan and Oswald are stupid and insulting.

Unfortunately, they're also very common. Liberal blogger Greg Sargent at the *Washington Post* put it this way: "Not to state the obvious or anything, but right-wing terrorists have been known to kill American citizens." The point was so obvious, in fact, that he didn't feel the need to list any examples. You know—like the Unibomber. Oh wait—he was a loony lefty.

Like Bill Ayers and the other Weather Underground bombers— uh, no . . .

I mean, Raymond Luc Levasseur, a.k.a. "New York City's most prolific bomber," whose terror group, United Freedom Front, killed a New Jersey state trooper as part of its Marxist—oops!

Hey, how about those Earth Liberation Front eco-whackjobs who burn down homes, scientific laboratories, and car dealersh...er, maybe not.

Okay, I'll admit, with a population of 300 million, America has actually produced a few rightwing domestic terrorists. I'll grant that Timothy McVeigh fits the bill, and so does Eric Rudolph, who bombed the 1996 Olympics, and possibly Scott Roeder, the killer of Kansas abortionist George Tiller.

But in recent decades, America has seen far more acts of terrorism and political violence from the Left than the Right. In addition to the leftwing terrorists mentioned above, we've seen politically motivated bank robberies,

Love Letter from the Left

"When Hamas does it or Hezbollah does it, it is called terrorism. Why should Republican lawmakers and the Astroturf groups organizing on behalf of the healthcare industry be viewed differently?"

—Keith Olbermann

kidnappings, shootings, and/or murders committed by the Black Panthers, the Symbionese Liberation Army, FALN, the Black Liberation Army, the May 19th Communist Organization, and other leftwing misfits.

Another big difference is that the Right typically rejects its own kooks—really, how many conservatives hail Timothy McVeigh? Meanwhile, the Left's relationship with its own violent extremists is much more...well, I guess they would call it "nuanced." The academic Left rewarded Weather Underground leader Bernardine Dohrn with a professorship at Northwestern University. Her husband, Bill Ayers, even got tenure at the University of Illinois, and he helped launch the political career of a certain well-known community organizer. Furthermore, a few months before leaving office, Bill Clinton commuted the sentences of sixteen members of FALN, a Puerto Rican terrorist group responsible for more than a hundred domestic bombings. And on his last day as president, Clinton sprung from jail Weather Underground terrorists Linda Sue Evans and Susan Rosenberg.

You won't see conservative academics (if there are any) hiring abortion clinic bombers, and you won't see conservative presidents letting them out of jail. That's because conservatives are hardly ever violent, and the few violent ones get denounced and ostracized. Yet the Obama Left obsessively decries non-existent rightwing violence. Where normal people see citizens expressing opinions at townhalls and on talk radio, liberals see wild-eyed mobs just one Rush Limbaugh monologue away from shooting up the local shopping mall.

The media coverage of the tea parties and townhalls was rife with insinuations that crowds were dangerously unruly. Video of cowardly congressmen sneaking out back doors to avoid their own citizens were used by CNN & Co. to imply that democracy was endangered by violent, rightwing mobs. Meanwhile, most normal people watching panic-stricken politicians flee a roomful of angry voters probably thought, "Well, it's about damn time."

Rightwing Violence: The Phantom Menace

Now, I'll concede there were a few violent incidents at tea parties and townhalls. A black man in St. Louis was beaten by a group of white thugs and sent to the hospital; an attendee at a union-sponsored event was punched for expressing his opinions; a Florida protester was beaten with a sign in the middle of the street; and one peaceful activist had his finger bitten off his hand by a counter-protester. (No—it wasn't *that* finger.)

What did all these attacks have in common? The victims were the "rightwingers," and all the attackers were O-bots.

The most egregious example was the case of Kenneth Gladney. He was just a guy trying to make a buck selling "Don't Tread on Me" flags outside a St. Louis townhall. Gladney, who is black, was beaten and stomped by mostly white SEIU union thugs at Congressman Russ Carnahan's townhall meeting in August 2009.

Needless to say, if Gladney had been an O-bot and white tea partiers had sent him to the hospital, it would have been a front-page story. Instead, the mainstream media largely ignored it, and despite the fact that Gladney's beating was caught on videotape, local prosecutors took nearly four months to file charges against his assailants.

Mary Katherine Ham analyzed the reports of violence at these events for the *Weekly Standard* in September 2009. Here's what she found:

In more than 400 events: one slap, one shove, three punches, two signs grabbed, one self-inflicted vandalism incident by a liberal, one unsolved vandalism incident, and one serious assault. Despite the left's insistence on the essentially barbaric nature of Obamacare critics, the video, photographic, and police report evidence is fairly clear in showing that 7 of the 10 incidents were perpetrated by Obama supporters and union members on Obama critics. If you add a phoned death threat to Democrat representative Brad Miller of N.C., from an Obama-care critic, the tally is 7 of 11.

In other words, there was hardly any violence at all in "The Summer of the Angry White Male"—and a majority of the punches were landed by leftwingers.

So what's behind the distorted image of "violent" tea partiers? That's easy: political intimidation. When Obama's top advisor, David Axelrod, told CBS that he worried the tea party protests "could mutate into something that's unhealthy," he was trying to squelch dissent. And the media are happy to pile on, as the *Christian Science Monitor* did by running a story about Axelrod's comments with the headline, "Axelrod comment that tea parties are 'unhealthy' stokes militia fears."

Militia fears? The article suggested the White House's attacks on tea partiers might drive them into the arms of violent militia groups. That means regular Americans like my mom can't win; if you're a conservative activist, you're a nut. And if you're not a nut, then being called a nut will eventually turn you into one.

You've probably never met a militia member in your life, but Democrats seem to think they dominate tea parties from coast to coast. During the healthcare debate, Rhode Island Democratic senator Sheldon Whitehouse exclaimed, "[The GOP] are desperate to break this president. They have ardent supporters who are nearly hysterical at the very election of President Barack Obama. The Birthers, the fanatics, the people running around in right-wing militia and Aryan support groups, it is unbearable to them that President Barack Obama should exist."

Wow. Rightwing militias...fanatics...Aryans. I had no idea Providence, Rhode Island, was home to the Fourth Reich.

Nancy Pelosi has been working from the same playbook. As tea party protests spread nationwide, Pelosi was asked whether "antigovernment rhetoric" could spark violence. Pelosi choked up as she recalled some disturbing events in her native San Francisco:

> I have concerns about some of the language that is being used because I saw this, myself, in the late '70s in San Francisco. This kind of rhetoric was very frightening, and it created a climate in which violence took place. And so I wish that we would all, again, curb our enthusiasm in some of the statements that are made, understanding that some of the people—the ears that it is falling on are not as balanced as the person making the statement might assume.

Pelosi was referring to the 1978 murders of San Francisco mayor George Moscone and city supervisor Harvey Milk. And this would be a compelling argument if there had been any rightwingers or antigovernment activists involved. But in fact, Moscone and Milk were killed by deranged former city councilor Dan White, a Democrat who was enraged by Moscone's refusal to reappoint him to his job. A fascinating story and a tragic crime—and one that has absolutely nothing to do with tea partiers or antigovernment rhetoric.

But liberals don't care. They're going to find rightwing violence, and they're not going to be deterred by trivialities—like the fact that there is none. In 2009, when the body of a census taker was found hanging from a tree in Kentucky with the word "fed" scrawled on his chest, liberals on MSNBC and elsewhere immediately declared him a victim of rightwing antigovernment violence. The *Village Voice* called his death part of the "rage against Washington...especially in the rural South," with "all the makings of some anti-government goober taking his half-wit beliefs way too far." Liberal blogger Boye' A. Coker wrote at Examiner.com,

> ## Love Letter from the Left
>
> "What I don't want to do is create an opportunity for the people who are political terrorists to blow up the meeting and not try to answer thoughtful questions."
>
> —Democratic Congressman Baron Hill, on opponents of ObamaCare

This is another prime example of how the right has lost it and the followers of Glenn Beck, Michelle [sic] Bachman [sic] and Rush Limbaugh et al, are merely responding to the incendiary and misguided "call to arms."

...It does not take much for one of these nut-wings with already diagnosed chemical imbalances [that would be *you*, my fellow conservatives—mg] to tip over to the other side and do something that Michelle [sic] Bachman [sic] et al may indeed come to regret.

Largely ignored were the facts on the ground: the police had yet to rule the census taker's death a homicide, and the man had a suspicious life insurance policy. The outrage poured out for a few weeks, until police ruled the case a suicide: the "victim" faked his own murder in order to get an insurance settlement for his son.

How sad—no, how outrageously unfair—that the manufactured storyline of rightwing violence is so well known that a desperate dad thought it would provide cover for his suicide.

And that was no isolated incident. In August 2009, after a vandal smashed windows at a Democratic Party office in Denver, the head of the Colorado Democrats, Pat Waak, immediately blamed rightwing opponents of Obama's healthcare plans. So it was very inconvenient when police later pinned the crime on a whacked out, transgendered leftwing activist, Maurice Schwenkler.

Has it occurred to any fair-minded Obama supporters that, if rightwing violence was actually a problem, leftwingers wouldn't have to keep making up examples? Nobody had to lie to prove that Bill Clinton had a (ahem) "pants" problem. All we had to do was name names. And there were lots of them.

But paranoid lefties have to keep making up cases of "tea partiers gone wild" because they have no true case to make. The accusation of violence is a way to stop debate and to avoid answering those hard, common-sense questions that people like my mom keep asking.

Look at it this way: these days, liberal politicians frequently hear questions like, "How is the same government that can't run Cash for Clunkers going to run the entire health system?" Increasingly, the answer we get is, "Run for your lives—it's a violent rightwing nut looking for a rifle and a clock tower!" And as long as that's the answer, typical Americans can't possibly understand Team Obama's real plans.

Then again, maybe that's the whole point.

Spot the *Real* Terrorist

Having organized several tea parties myself, I have to confess that the portrayal of tea partiers as dangerous radicals plotting violent revolution is, well, hilarious. Have you seen the people who show up to these rallies? I mean, I love you, my fellow tea partiers, you are my people, but—c'mon. Violent revolutionaries? Radical terrorists?

Please.

Fashion terrorists, maybe. I doubt the typical tea partier is going to run amok in the halls of government, but many appear to have done so in the aisles of Wal-Mart. Half an hour into one townhall event, I wanted to grab the mic and announce, "Hey, guys—when girls wear shirts that stop half way down their bodies, they're called 'belly shirts.' When *you* do, it's called 'morbid obesity.' Drop the twinkies and head to the XXXL aisle, now!"

The rest of the crowd is dominated by mild-mannered middle Americans, including lots of older folks. These people wouldn't riot if you held a gun on them. In fact, if you *did* hold a gun on them, you'd most likely get a polite lecture on proper firearm etiquette.

These aren't political radicals. They're the people of the hotdish. They politely wait their turn to shout their slogans. And after they're done with their "threatening" tirades supposedly calling for the imposition of a white, Christian fascist regime, these alleged domestic jihadists pick up all the litter on their way home. Many bring their own recycling bags. The only way to whip them into a violent frenzy would be by telling them you were responsible for cancelling *Matlock*.

Otherwise, forget it. There is no significant element among tea partiers that can compare with their leftwing counterparts who trash just about every venue whenever a few world leaders get together. And yet, the media show a curious sympathy for the leftist thugs, even though they destroy property, hurt policemen, and engage in other acts of violence. But if some frustrated town-hall attendees yell at their lying congressman, the O-bots want to turn the water cannons on the crowd and then lock them up for sedition.

And there are no signs at tea party rallies that come close to the violent incitement that was routinely found at anti-Bush rallies—signs like "We Support Our Troops When They Shoot Their Officers," "Death to Extremist Terrorist Christian Pig Bush," and "Support the Iraqi Resistance."

Of course, every man-hour the government spends snooping around my dad's RV looking for a telltale copy of *Atlas Shrugged* is an hour that could have been spent investigating other things—like *real* terrorists. And as it turns out, around the same time the DHS released its report on rightwing terrorism, a real domestic terrorist was plotting to kill Americans. According to the *Washington Post*,

> [I]nvestigators came across Internet postings, allegedly by [Nadil M.] Hasan, that indicated sympathy for suicide bombers and empathized with the plight of Muslim civilians killed in Iraq and Afghanistan, according to a federal official briefed on the situation. The official, and another source, said investigators never confirmed whether Hasan was the author of the postings and did not pursue the matter.

And what happened six months after investigators found these posts? Major Nidal Hasan unloaded about 100 rounds from two pistols at Fort Hood, Texas, killing twelve soldiers, one civilian, and an unborn baby, and wounding more than thirty others.

While talk radio listeners were being labeled potential terrorists for posting times and locations of upcoming townhall meetings, Hasan was uploading pro-suicide bombing messages onto the Internet. While concerned citizens were attending tea parties, Hasan was corresponding with a known al Qaeda supporter in Yemen who had served as a spiritual adviser to three of the 9/11 hijackers. While you were lecturing your congressman on the details of a healthcare bill he never read, Hasan was making quite an impression on his colleagues at Walter Reed hospital. According to a reporter for National Public Radio,

> [Hasan] seemed almost belligerent about being Muslim, and he gave a lecture one day that really freaked a lot of doctors out.
>
> …Hasan apparently gave a long lecture on the Koran and talked about how if you don't believe, you are condemned to hell. Your head is cut off. You're set on fire. Burning oil is burned down your throat.

The reporter added, "The psychiatrist I talked to today said that [Hasan] was the kind of guy who the staff actually stood around in the hallway, saying: Do you think he's a terrorist, or is he just weird?"

Hasan's colleagues were doctors, not terrorism investigators, and even they could see something was wrong with the guy. But the government couldn't see it. In fact, subsequent investigations found that Hasan was repeatedly promoted despite poor performance

and constant conflict with his fellow soldiers. He even kept his
security clearances after the military discovered his contact with
the al Qaeda goon in Yemen. How? Several offices speculated
that his superiors refused to call him out for fear of looking politically incorrect.

Meanwhile, how many alerts did the DHS issue about Hasan?
None. As Instapundit blogger Glenn Reynolds put it, "Too busy
worrying about Glenn Beck viewers, military veterans, and Tea
Party organizers, I guess."

Just two months later, a jihadist with ties to the same radical
imam who counseled Hasan got on an Amsterdam-to-Detroit
flight with a jockstrap full of explosives. Instead of handing this
al Qaeda-trained terrorist over to military intelligence, the Obama
administration chose to arrest him and give him the right to
remain silent.

When our politicians are more focused on the security "threat"
of angry taxpayers with policy questions than they are on radical
Muslims with access to weapons and U.S. military installations,
you know their priorities are out of whack. And the fact that a
jihadist on a government watch list can waltz onto a U.S.-bound
plane with his underwear full of explosives also indicates that
Homeland Security doesn't have its eye on the ball. Then again,
Muslim terrorists only kill *people*. Angry voters kill liberal political careers.

In the era of real-live terrorism, why work so hard to label folks
like my mom terrorists? It's all politics—pure Saul Alinsky stuff.
The trick is to marginalize your opponents by portraying them as
extreme, dangerous, or just strange. This is pretty effective, which
is why millions of Americans would never attend a tea party, even
though they share tea party ideals. They've been scared away, con-
vinced by the mainstream media that you're a bunch of kooks.

I wonder if the Left understands the impact this assault is having on typical Americans. Folks like my mom don't really like name-calling. When a presidential website calls them "antidemocratic" and "heirs of bin Laden," it makes them wonder what they've done wrong. They assume somebody, somewhere really means it. They don't know it's just pure Obama spin and Chicago-style intimidation.

And that's another big difference between tea partiers and left-wingers. Many folks on the Left—particularly among the ranks of angry pundits and fevered bloggers—take pride in being called "radical" or, even better, "dangerous." They'd be thrilled to be investigated by the Department of Homeland Security—particularly the old *Bush* Homeland Security. It would feed into their delusional fantasy that they're involved in a grand struggle against evil corporations and nefarious U.S. intelligence agencies. They would become instant martyrs for nationalized healthcare, welfare for polar bears, or whatever nutty cause they're championing that week.

Instead, when the DHS *did* issue a report on potential leftwing activities, Napolitano's crew focused narrowly on a handful of specific groups like eco-terrorists, mysteriously leaving out the broader leftwing community. Apparently, it's only the conservative movement that's comprised of "dangerous radicals" and potential terrorists.

What a surprise.

Happy Warriors

My mom's not going to like hearing this, but there's a reason aside from political expediency why the Obama elites demonize her and her fellow tea partiers: a lot of O-bots really believe America is an enemy camp full of racist would-be assassins. Our lefty friends genuinely fear that the guy with a "Don't Tell Obama What Comes After a Trillion" sign today will be shooting up motorcades tomorrow.

I fully realized this in late 2009 during the infamous "party crashers" incident at the White House. A Virginia couple from the polo-and-playgirl set, Tareq and Michaele Salahi, managed to get into President Obama's first state dinner without an invitation. They got into the reception line, had their photos taken with the president and vice president, and later posted the pictures on Facebook.

This caused an uproar about the incompetence of the Secret Service and White House social secretaries. But many pundits, including Mark Steyn, Charles Krauthammer, and myself, thought the story was a hoot. We liked the idea that a couple of clever, self-promoting, and completely harmless citizens could, using a well-tailored tux and a red-hot wife, finagle their way into the White House. After all, as I pointed out on the air, they were Americans.

My comments really brought out the crazy in my liberal listeners. As one caller told me, "You call yourself patriotic. I don't consider myself patriotic [there's a real shocker—mg], and I'm outraged....I hear violence in your words. The people who attack Obama as virulently as you and your friends can't tolerate his presidency." Do I really think President Obama was safe, he demanded, just because the crashers were Americans?

Yes, in fact I do. Americans who don't support the president's policies aren't looking to hurt anyone, least of all the president. The supposed violent tendencies of Obama's critics are fantasies dreamed up by people with unfulfilling lives. Sure, there are a few nuts out there who expect the streets to be filled with blue-helmeted soldiers dragging our daughters away for UN-mandated abortions. But America is a big country, and they are a tiny group. The effort to blur the clear-cut distinction between a handful of loonies on the one hand, and on the other, a huge, nationwide movement for responsible, limited government, is really a disgraceful con-job that the media, unfortunately, promotes at every turn.

I can tell you from personal experience that most tea partiers are pretty happy, contrary to the popular myth of the angry, dangerous radical. They oppose the current administration's tax-and-spend policies, so they spend an hour or two at a rally, then pick up the kids from soccer practice, have dinner, tuck everyone in bed, and then, drifting off to sleep, marvel at how they've been so blessed. They love their country and their family enough to fight for them by speaking out. It's that simple.

For normal folks like my mom, and for typical conservatives like my listeners, turning to violence contradicts their fundamental instincts. They debate politics, they care about this country deeply, but they don't view politics as an all-encompassing struggle. They don't need "the fight" to give meaning to their existence—they already have a life.

Chapter Three

America, He's Just Not That Into You

Among the many historic "firsts" accomplished the day Barack Obama was elected president, the most significant, I believe, is this: he's the first American president who doesn't actually like Americans.

Oh, sure, Andrew Jackson was a cranky, thin-skinned sort who liked to settle disputes with pistols at ten paces. And "Silent Cal" Coolidge may have been emotionally distant. Then there was Bill Clinton, who loved some Americans a little too much.

But Obama, who began as the Candidate of Cool, quickly transformed in office into the Ambassador of Aloof, the Deputy of Distant, the Commissar of Cold.

It's an odd thing to say about the leader of the free world, but sometimes Obama acts like he's got better things to do with his time—and better people to do it for.

This is something new. Let's face it—we spoiled Americans are used to political suck-ups. We expect our politicians to spend their time promising chickens in every pot, jobs for every illiterate, and money falling like manna from the sky—all without a tax increase or a dollar of debt.

As a native of the South, for example, I grew up with a certain breed of politician who understood the value of agreeing with everyone. He was that daring leader who, when confronted by a divisive proposal, would rise to his feet and declare boldly, "Some of the people are for it. Some are against it. And I'm with the people!"

This is definitely not the Obama way.

It's not that President Obama's promises are all realistic or that he always keeps them. (See "new era of transparency and accountability," "no lobbyists," "no tax hikes for earners under $250,000," "no increase in deficits," "broadcast healthcare negotiations on CSPAN," etc.) And it's not that he won't pander to an audience. He just won't pander to *us*.

But watch him bow to Saudi sheiks and the Japanese emperor. He practically scrapes the floor before them. Watch the YouTube clips of Obama talking about America to audiences abroad. There are so many Euroweenies who want to revel in America's shortcomings, and our president is happy to oblige.

Has a national political figure from either party ever talked about the American people the way President Obama has? Since the earliest days of his candidacy, Obama has repeatedly reminded the American people that we're letting him down. And he's not happy about it, either.

Oh sure, ask him his views on America as a country, the ol' "amber waves of grain, purple mountains majesty," and he's just fine. But ask him about the people who actually live here— particularly in the parts between Boston and the San Francisco Bay—and he's got a serious attitude problem.

You remember his off-the-record description of rural Pennsyl- vanians at a San Francisco fundraiser during the 2008 primary? "So it's not surprising then that they get bitter, they cling to guns or religion or antipathy to people who aren't like them or anti-immi- grant sentiment or anti-trade sentiment as a way to explain their frustrations." This from a guy who's campaigning for our votes?

I think Obama has made an even more revealing comment, one that didn't attract much attention. Speaking to a group of far-Left supporters, then Senator Obama heard his political allies bashing the ideas and actions of average Americans—hardly out of the ordinary. But realizing the cameras were on, he valiantly leapt to our defense:

> The one thing that I want to insist on is that, as I travel
> around the country, the American people are a decent people.
> Now they get confused sometimes. You know, they listen to
> the wrong talk radio shows or watch the wrong TV net-
> works, but they're basically decent, they're basically sound.

Basically decent? *Basically* sound? Please, Mr. President—you're making me blush!

A Different Kind of President

When the Obama administration announced that 9/11 master- mind Khalid Sheik Mohammed would be given a civilian trial in a New York federal court with all the rights of a U.S. citizen, an attorney friend called me in a rage.

"What the hell is the president doing?" he demanded. "This is insane. Who is he trying to impress by dragging that [expletive deleted] to New York?" He continued, "My friends and I have been talking about it all day. It doesn't make any sense. I don't know anybody who thinks this is a good idea. Nobody!"

Ah, but you don't know anyone like Barack Obama.

In fact, hardly anybody does. Forget skin color. The real divide between President Obama and the average American relates to ideology and experience. There just aren't many Americans of any race, creed, or color who've lived a life like Obama's.

How many people, black or white, do you know who were raised by their mother and grandmother in Hawaii and Indonesia? How many people do you know whose father was a bigamist? How many community organizers do you know? Not people who work at nonprofits, or fundraise, or volunteer; I mean people whose career has been ideological activism and who've never had what most of us would consider a real job. Anyone?

How many of your friends even know a former domestic terrorist like Bill Ayers, much less worked with one or started their political career at the guy's house? Do you know anyone who would attend a church led by the Reverend Jeremiah Wright more than once? How about for twenty years?

In 2004, Barack Obama was by all accounts an undistinguished member of the Illinois state legislature, casting votes (often "present") on mundane issues like road maintenance budgets and declaring the Official State Fruit. (It's the goldrush apple.) Just four years later he was the President-elect of the United States, about to decide issues of war, homeland security, and economic policy for the most powerful nation in the history of the world. Who do you know who's moved up so far, so fast? His campaign featured a massive rally of his supporters in Berlin. As in Germany. Who else has run a campaign like that?

When *People* magazine reported in 2008 that Obama doesn't give his daughters Christmas or birthday presents, my talk show phone lines lit up with a bipartisan group of bewildered parents asking, "What's the deal with that?" Even his own daughter, revealing to *Access Hollywood* that her dad doesn't like ice cream, insisted, "Everybody should like ice cream."

I'm not saying all these aspects of Obama's biography are bad. I'm just saying they're *different*—different from the life experience of any other president and from the vast majority of Americans.

We've had rich presidents and poor ones, smart ones and dumb ones, urban mayors and country legislators. We've had crooks and hacks and heroes and leaders. But there has never been a president who had as little in common with the citizens he governs as Barack Obama.

Now, when it comes to presidents and their people, differences don't necessarily mean distance. Was movie star Ronald Reagan really a common man? Could Richie-Rich FDR possibly relate to the travails of the little guy?

But President Obama is distanced from Americans by more than his unusual background—there's an ideological gulf as well. The most liberal president in American history is governing a center-right nation—one that has become even more conservative since he became president, according to polls.

Take these basic differences in politics and personal life, and is it any wonder that Team Obama always seems so surprised by public opposition to its policies? Since Obama's inauguration, Americans haven't known what to make of this president, as he and his allies struggle to grasp the values and concerns of average Americans.

Obama's team was surprised by the widespread opposition to the stimulus package, which failed to get any GOP support in the House. (Or create jobs, for that matter.) It was thrown off by the negative reaction to its calls to close Guantanamo Bay and to investigate CIA interrogators. Healthcare "reform" was supposed to be a popular, bipartisan success—wrong again. And the O-bots seemed genuinely taken aback by the ridicule Janet Napolitano earned when she replaced the word "terrorism" with "man-caused disasters." They didn't even see the outrage coming when she insisted that a Muslim terrorist's ability to board a U.S.-bound flight with explosives sewed into his underwear somehow proved that "the system worked."

These battles weren't between Obama and the Republican opposition as much as they were between the president and We, the People. In January 2009, President-elect Obama could walk on water and part the seas. A year later, the unpopularity of his policies was bringing down his whole party. ObamaCare was dead in the water, and Congressional Democrats were in open revolt against Obama's signature plans for a cap-and-trade carbon trading scheme. Democratic congressmen began announcing their impending retirements, while Alabama Democrat Parker Griffith went over to the GOP. Having provided the final vote to pass Obama's healthcare reform in the Senate, Nebraska Democrat Ben Nelson saw his popularity bottom out in his home state. In December, the number of Americans identifying themselves as Democrats fell to a seven-year low in a Rasmussen poll. For Pete's sake, a Democrat couldn't even get elected to statewide offices in the true-blue states of New Jersey and Massachusetts.

This sure wasn't the result of brilliant Republican Party leadership. It was due to millions of regular Americans who called congressmen, emailed senators, and marched in their home towns. It was due to people like my mom.

We, the Problem

When President Obama and his allies look out across the "Great Unwashed" (a phrase surely well-known in this White House), they don't see allies. They see obstacles. They see people who distrust the government and want more autonomy from it. They see people who want to create wealth rather than redistribute it.

They see Americans who mostly like their jobs and their doctors, Americans who buy the cars they want, live where they want, and eat the food they want, whether New York mayor Michael Bloomberg approves or not.

They see Americans who believe in individual responsibility—which means they will let their neighbor fail if he deserves it. But that sense of responsibility is tempered by compassion—they will reach out to help him if he deserves it, too. They actually believe people should pay their own bills, take charge of their own healthcare, and raise their own kids. Americans' vision of "social justice" isn't "everyone getting what they want." It's people getting what they earn—the good and the bad.

And for the Obama elites, these attitudes are a problem.

The O-bots want to fundamentally change what it means to be an American. No, they aren't al Qaeda agents or Communist spies working off a forged Kenyan birth certificate, or any of that other nonsense. But they *are* engaged in a coordinated and extremely dangerous assault against the American character. This isn't a fight over public policy. It's a fight over people's attitudes, over our values and beliefs.

During the healthcare debate in summer 2009, the O-bots began asking why their idol was facing such resistance. Many of his supporters said the president was running into the wall of racism at the center of the American character. They were half right.

President Obama hit a wall, but it's not prejudice or racism. It's the essential values most Americans uphold. That's why he's not content with changing policies; he must "remake" America. He aims to "fix" our "broken" souls, to transform our nation so that we can't go back to our old lives. He wants to forge a new nation of which Michelle Obama can finally be proud.

You probably recognize these comments by our president and First Lady. Consider for a moment how profoundly negative they all are toward the fundamental nature of America and its people.

It's hard to imagine another president or his wife repudiating America so definitively. Then again, who can imagine another president spending twenty years worshipping in a church whose preacher denounces the "U.S. of KKKA?" Or one who grumbles that not enough of us speak Spanish, or who insists that we can no longer expect to "drive whatever car we want," and "set our thermostats" how we like?

When Barack Obama made these comments, he wasn't calling for a National Department of Thermostat Monitoring and Maintenance, or suggesting some other mere policy change. He was trashing the American character.

And he's not alone. A fairly large contingent on the Left views the American people as suspect and our belief in American exceptionalism as dangerous. The fringiest of these folks believe that American agents actually blew up the buildings on 9/11 or allowed the attacks to happen. And many others proclaim that America brought 9/11 upon itself. To quote President Obama's long-time pastor, they think "America's chickens had come home to roost."

I don't know if Barack and Michelle Obama were in their pews the Sunday after 9/11, when Reverend Wright made that egregious, disgusting comment. I'd like to think that, if they were, they got up and walked out.

But I do know from watching the video that nobody attending Trinity United Church of Christ that day was offended enough to leave. The people in President Obama's congregation didn't find the comments particularly outrageous.

And why should they? Similar sentiments were expressed by Upper West Side liberals in the *New York Times*, by college professors, and by others across the leftwing spectrum. For the kind of folks President Obama hangs out with, denouncing America is just another day at the community activism office.

As a candidate, Obama repeatedly argued that America's fundamental character was flawed: too much selfishness, not enough spreading the wealth. "Let us be our brother's keeper," said a man whose half-brother was living in squalor on $1 a month in Kenya at that very moment,

Love Letter from the Left

"God damn America, that's in the Bible for killing innocent people. God damn America for treating our citizens as less than human. God damn America for as long as she acts like she is God and she is supreme."

—Reverend Jeremiah Wright

and whose aunt was living illegally on the taxpayer dole in a Boston housing project.

Brother-keeping is a longstanding tradition here in America, the most generous nation in the world. According to a Hudson Institute study, in 2007 Americans gave $115.9 billion in private donations and remittances to the developing world, more than five times the amount of U.S. government aid. Interestingly, Professor Arthur C. Brooks, author of *Who Really Cares*, found that political conservatives—a.k.a. "those most likely to oppose President Obama's policies"—give 30 percent more to charities than their liberal counterparts.

That's the American way. And that's the president's problem. He needs a nation of stingy, uncaring jerks so he can transform us—through the healing power of government, Hallelujah!—into a better country. It screws up his whole plan if we simply help people out on our own.

Worse, if we believe we have an individual duty to aid a brother or sister in need, and if churches and private charities are going to help people without a government mandate, then there's no need for the Federal Department of Need-Based Brother and Sister Assistance, East Coast Division, Atlantic Region, Coastal Area, Office J127A.

Europeans have lots of bureaucracies like this. They also give less to charity, help fewer people around the world, and are much less hard-working than Americans. And we now have a president who wants us to be more like them.

If you believe that America is great and has the capacity to become even greater, then you don't need fundamental change. If you believe in American exceptionalism, that this nation is "the last, best hope of man on earth," then you're building on our traditions, not trying to tear them down.

If, on the other hand, you sincerely believe that the only thing exceptional about America is that its people are exceptionally dangerous, backward, and just plain dumb...well, then you're gonna need a really good stump speech when you run for office.

If you honestly think we'd be a better nation if we were less exceptional and more like Europe, less dedicated to individual responsibility and more committed to collectivism, less like the old West and more like the UN—then you need more than the same old politics. The usual promises to adjust the tax rates or amend the Clean Air Act won't cut it.

You need hope and change. You need change to come. You need change we can believe in, change you can count on, change you can find in your sofa. You need a change in attitudes, a change in values, a change in the weather, and a change in the sea. A change in you and a change in me. You need to be the change you've been waiting for. You need change, change, CHANGE!

Sound familiar?

And because Obama and his hard-Left allies are determined to change far more than policy, they've made the current struggle into a debate over people. They aren't fighting an ideology, they're fighting individuals. Put another way, it's not your politics or your principles that are the problem. It's *you*.

Think back—when was the last time you heard President Obama or his spokesmen condemn a specific Republican congressman or senator? Have you ever heard him insult the intelligence of, say, Republican Senate leader Mitch McConnell? Can you recall a White House spokesflak making snide remarks about John Boehner?

I can't remember it happening. But how many times did the Obama elites trash Joe the Plumber? And how many insults has Team Obama hurled at everyday citizens who showed up at tea parties and townhalls? Too many to count. Forget "I'm with the people." Obama sounds more like legendary Democratic pol Dick Tuck who, after losing a race for California state senate, famously declared, "The people have spoken—the bastards."

I'm not saying President Obama thinks we're all a bunch of, well, you know. But on a basic level, he clearly sees the American character as a problem to be solved.

Contrast this to the attitude of the previous "transformative" president, Ronald Reagan, who proclaimed, "Government is not the solution to our problem. Government *is* the problem." With this affirmation, Reagan was saying something about the character of the American people. He was expressing his confidence in his fellow citizens, his belief that, if left to our own devices, we would more often than not make our lives better, our families stronger, and our nation greater. It was too much government interference in our lives that hurt us, not a lack thereof.

Now try to imagine President "Community Organizer," President "Netroots," President "Yes, We Can" Obama making that statement. Would he say, "Government is the problem and individuals expressing their free choices are the solution?" Would he say it ever? Even back when he still smoked pot?

No way. For President Obama, it's the other way 'round. He imagines all the wonderful things government could do—heal the sick, enrich the poor, name more public schools after a certain Nobel Laureate—if only the "confused but basically decent" people would just get out of his way.

Free-thinkers, Unite (to Stamp Out Dissent)

Rather than unleashing the power of free minds and free markets, President Obama seeks to unleash the government at every "problem" he can find: your private-sector doctor, your privately owned business, your privately earned wealth, your privately purchased SUV.

He already has the government running car companies, setting salaries for CEOs, and regulating your light bulbs. And he wants the government to do a million other new things, from slapping a "sin tax" on your soda pop to dictating the country's entire carbon output. And what's stopping him from fulfilling this big-government vision?

My mom—with some help from millions of other Americans who wish the president well but absolutely reject his vision of the world. People who refuse to go quietly into that good nightmare of a Euro-style, nanny-state America.

And why won't we?

President Obama thinks it's because we're dumb. I say it's because we're paying attention. Seriously—you have to have an incredibly low opinion of the abilities of your fellow Americans to believe they are less competent than the DMV or the IRS.

When President Obama talks about government-run "public options" bringing savings, efficiency, and improved service to healthcare, for example, the typical American who's familiar with government "efficiency" looks at him like a dog listening to opera. "What the hell is he talking about? And where's my bacon?"

When we hear "government-run," we think of headlines like "$3 billion Cash for Clunkers program fails to turn around car market," and "Four-year-old receives government mortgage bailout check," and "Federal workers busted for spending thousands of work hours surfing porn."

Does President Obama really believe we'd be better off with more of that? Does he honestly think the American family is a bigger mess than Boston's Big Dig?

In a word, yes.

He is absolutely certain that more government "guidance" would improve our lives and that we disagree only because, well, we're dim bulbs to start with. For example, during the 2009 healthcare debate, Obama told an audience of Democrats, "Democrats are an opinionated bunch. You know, the other side, they just kinda sometimes do what they're told. Democrats, y'all thinkin' for yourselves."

Got the message? You conservatives are obedient, mind-numbed robots (to borrow Rush's phrase), while Obama's liberal allies are independent, open-minded free thinkers. This, of course, is evidenced by:

- the Democrats' lock-step, partisan voting record
- the O-bots' attempts to squelch all dissent by labeling it "racism"
- liberals teaching school children to sing songs praising their Dear Leader in the White House
- the White House establishing the "fishy@white-house.gov" website to track dissenting emails
- the Obama flacks' attacks on FOX News for reporting stories they don't like
- the administration setting up a taxpayer-funded website that sends citizens' letters of support to President Obama

Call it "free thinking, North Korea-style."

Why the insults from Obama? Does he acknowledge *any* legitimate, thoughtful reasons why someone might not support ObamaCare? Maybe I can help him out. Here are a few items that hit the news the very same week Obama described Republican dissent as mindless obedience:

- The estimated price tag for ObamaCare jumped to $1 trillion.
- Unemployment claims surged by another half million, and one of President Obama's top economic advisors, Christina Romer, said the impact of Obama's stimulus package had likely peaked—more bad news for businesses nervous about the cost of ObamaCare.
- The British press reported the socialized National Health Service has spent more than 1.5 million pounds ($2.4 million) since 2007 so that more than 3,000 of its medical workers could bypass its own waiting lists and get private healthcare.

And there are a lot more perfectly reasonable concerns that cause people to ask, "Hey, is this ObamaCare thing a smart move?" So why did Obama immediately insist that Republicans were voting "no" because Dick Cheney called from the bunker and told them to?

His assumption says nothing about the actual motives of his opponents, but it speaks volumes about what he thinks of you and me.

Try this analogy: if a husband surprises his wife with a diamond necklace, she might wonder why he did it. It could be because he was simply overcome by his love for her. Or perhaps he found one of his secretary's earrings in his car, realized the other one was in the pocket of the suit his wife just took to the cleaners, and found himself in need of an extravagant gesture of apology.

His wife doesn't know why he bought it. But if her first instinct when she gets the necklace is to blurt out, "Okay, Buster, what have you been up to?" then you know what she thinks of her husband's character.

The same goes for President Obama and his allies. Their first assumption in every policy debate is that their opponents are acting with bad motives. Opposing ObamaCare means you're a "stooge of the insurance industry." Noting that Obama has abandoned a lot of campaign pledges equals "being uncomfortable with a black president." Opposing wildly expensive cap and trade plans proves you're "in bed with the oil companies."

And so when Rick Santelli unleashed the famous diatribe that helped usher in the tea party movement, he became a primary target of the Obama White House. "I'm not entirely sure where Mr. Santelli lives or in what house he lives," sniffed Obama spokes-hack Robert Gibbs. He continued, "I also think it's extremely important for people who rant on cable television to be responsible and understand what

Love Letter from the Left

"You crazy sons-of-b*tches, you right-wingers. Do you not understand that the people you hold up as heroes bombed your G*ddamn country? Do you not understand that Glenn Beck and Sean Hannity and Rush Limbaugh and Bill O'Reilly are as complicit of the September 11, 2001, terror attack as any one of those dumb-ass fifteen who came from Saudi Arabia? Don't you get that?"

—liberal talk host Mike Malloy

they're talking about. I feel assured that Mr. Santelli doesn't understand what he's talking about."

Of course not. Rick Santelli's a successful financial professional who disagrees with the Obama administration. He must, therefore, be an idiot. Or worse. A *New York Times* blog reprinted these comments from O-bot blogger Charles Lumos:

> After watching the [Santelli clip], I first had to check my calendar. Somehow I felt I traveled back in time to the early 1970s to witness first hand Richard Nixon's "northern strategy," his pursuit of white ethnic voters who were so deeply disaffected over Great Society programs ranging from desegregation (remember the Boston busing madness?) to affirmative action among others that they would desert the Democratic Party becoming "Nixon's silent majority" and "Reagan Democrats."
>
> …Rick Santelli is heir to this legacy laced with racist overtones….It's back to the 1970s for the GOP and their rabid white ethnics.
>
> I spent a decade on Wall Street working for Alex. Brown & Sons, Deutsche Banc Securities and Goldman Sachs. I found Wall Street a largely liberal environment with one major exception, the trading floor. In my experience I found traders, who are largely white ethnics—Irish, Italian, Greek, Polish or Slovak among others—and graduates of the Seton Halls, the Boston Colleges, the Notre Dames, the Penn States were the most rabid conservative and foul mouthed people on the planet. Nor could any of them ever get my name right. "My name is Charles, not Chuckie" was something I would repeat whenever I had the misfortune to have to interact with them. Some of these folks made William Buckley appear moderate.

Got that, you racist Notre Dame grads? You're gonna pay for $800,000 mortgages taken out by school bus drivers who couldn't afford them—and you're gonna LIKE it! Just keep your "racist overtones" to yourselves, you EYE-talians and Penn State fans. We liberal progressives know the *real* reason you don't support Obama. It's because you're bigots, you bunch of goat-chasing, knuckle-dragging Slavs! So shut up, swallow higher taxes, choke down another bailout, pay your neighbor's mortgage, and get with the program!

Aren't all political debates like this, you may ask? And the answer for any fair-minded person is "no." Consider the tea parties and townhalls where folks opposed these liberal proposals for massive new spending, new debt, and new government intrusions into the private sector. How many people stood up and insisted there was something intrinsically wrong with their congressman for supporting this? How many asked, "Why are you, Congressman So-and-So, such a bad person?"

It happened—but not often. The overwhelming message of the loyal Obama opposition is simply this: "You're wrong on the issue." Sure, some liberal pols support big government for dubious reasons—say, because their backers in Big Labor like it. And thick-necked SEIU members have been known to spread that message through, er, "hands-on" communications. But most ObamaCare opponents assume their congressman supported the plan because he genuinely believed in the policy.

Compare that to what your president had to say about *you* on the eve of Congress's vote to pass ObamaCare. A *New York Times* blog reported,

> Mr. Obama, during his private pep talk to Democrats...
> posed a question to the other lawmakers. According to

Representative Earl Blumenauer of Oregon, who supports the health care bill, the president asked, "Does anybody think that the teabag, anti-government people are going to support them if they bring down health care? All it will do is confuse and dispirit" Democratic voters "and it will encourage the extremists."

"Teabag, antigovernment extremists?" Thank you for your kind words, Mr. President.

Here's the main difference between us Obama infidels and the O-bots: we separate people's politics from their personal morality. O-bots, however, believe your politics define your morality. That means if you disagree with their agenda, you're either a corporate dupe or a racist. In their eyes, you can be an inveterate adulterer or a high-dollar tax cheat overseeing the IRS, and you still get to claim the moral high ground as long as you're a scumbag on "their side" of the healthcare debate.

Every American president has spoken out against his rivals. But I can't think of another president who treated typical citizens this way—not even Nixon, who at least confined his enemies list mostly to big-name political opponents. No administration before Obama's has cried "Hater!" and released the dogs of war upon the general population. Trashing politicians is good fun. But political attacks against the American people? That's a new low.

After all, what did we do?

Joe the Plumber asked Obama a challenging question about his tax policy. For that, Joe was pilloried by the Obama-worshipping press and had personal information leaked by government hacks.

Frank the Firefighter, one of eighteen New Haven firefighters who had their promotion exam cancelled because the group that passed it wasn't "diverse" enough, was flayed by blogging O-bots as a racist and also had details of his personal life used against him.

And then there's *you*. If you're a talk radio listener, or if you attended a townhall or tea party, you've been trashed, too—as you well know. And there's a whole lot of you out there—48 million talk radio listeners, according to Arbitron ratings. As Randall Bloomquist at Talk Frontier.com notes, "That's a pretty big group to dismiss as a 'fringe.'" Now add the five million Americans who, by my count, have attended a tea party or townhall meeting since spring 2009. Obviously those two groups overlap, but it's reasonable to assume that attacking these groups means you're attacking some 50 million Americans, most of them very likely voters.

Why would any politician do that? Even if you think Americans are a bunch of bigoted morons, why would you tell them that? Think of it this way: if you're one of Obama's political handlers, and you saw millions of passionate voters taking to the streets, would you have your partisans insult them by labeling them racist extremists? In a democracy, it's sheer political stupidity. But that's exactly what Team Obama has done.

Instead of attacking and demonizing them, wouldn't it be better to engage the anxious citizens and try to find some common ground? By showing some concern and sympathy, you might even get them on board with you—or at least defuse some of their energetic opposition.

Okay, if you can see the wisdom of that approach, why can't the Smartest President Ever® see it? It's smart politics to co-opt your opponents, and it's dumb politics to attack the great mass of American people. But Obama loves to attack his opponents, especially everyday Americans who go to tea parties. Why? Because he doesn't want to persuade you. He wants to defeat you. You're not his citizens, his public, or even his servants. You're his problem.

When he talks about "change," he's talking about changing what it fundamentally means to be an American. He's talking about repairing the "flawed" character of the American people.

He's talking about you.

Either You're with Obama, or You're with the Racists

From the beginning of his presidential campaign, Obama has presented himself as a test case on the character of his fellow Americans. After winning the Iowa caucus, he called his victory the "moment when we beat back the politics of fear and doubt and cynicism"—as though only scared, doubting cynics would oppose the presidential candidacy of a half-term senator with no executive, military, or business experience.

And the liberals who suspect (and some who openly proclaim) that most Americans are selfish, bigoted dolts, have amplified that message. They divided America into two groups: people who support Obama and his policies on the one hand, and racist holdouts on the other.

You're either with the plan, or in the Klan.

And so, when Obama lost the New Hampshire primary to Hillary Clinton in January 2008, the media immediately declared it a victory—not for Hillary, but for racism. Did it matter that Obama was virtually unknown just three months earlier? That he had won his first big victory in Iowa just days earlier? That he was running against Hillary Clinton, one of the best-known Democrats in America, who had campaigned hard in the Granite State?

Nope. The voters of New Hampshire—the *Democratic primary voters*—had failed this test of their character. They weren't concerned citizens with reasonable worries about Obama's lack of experience. They weren't voters who preferred Hillary's message. No, they were bad people. There was something wrong with them.

Obama supporters immediately claimed their fellow Democrats just weren't ready to vote for a black man. Chris Matthews continued the theme the next morning on MSNBC while discussing with Joe Scarborough why Obama's vote tally was lower than polls had projected:

> **Scarborough:** So what happened here?
>
> **Matthews:** Well, there's an old phrase in statistics—garbage in, garbage out. If the people don't tell the truth to the pollsters, they can't poll.
>
> **Scarborough:** Why wouldn't they tell the truth?
>
> **Matthews:** Well, remember Tonto and the Lone Ranger? Methinks Paleface speak with forked tongue.
>
> **Scarborough:** Yeah.
>
> **Matthews:** You hear me? Forked tongue.
>
> ...
>
> **Matthews:** I thought the lying would end with the wonderful performance of Harold Ford Jr., who beat the polling in Tennessee. I thought it ended with macaca. I thought white voters had stopped being what they didn't want to be. And you know what it tells me? People aren't proud of who they are. They're not proud of saying who they are. If they want to vote for Hillary Clinton, fine. Why don't they say so? Why don't they tell the pollsters that?

Scarborough: I'm used to people saying that we in the South have race problems.

Matthews: Ugh. Tell me about it.

Scarborough: But talk about New England.

Matthews: Boston? BOSTON?

Scarborough: Yeah. South Boston.

Matthews: Boston, the whole thing, the idea there's some—there's different kinds of prejudice, as you know, in the north than there is in the south, but it exists. It may not be "I think I'm better than you," but it might be "I don't want to live next door to you." There's different kinds of prejudices in this world. Let's face it.

Yes, let's face it: the same New Hampshire Democrats who handed victories to Al Gore, Paul Tsongas, and Jimmy Carter suddenly became backwater bigots. How? By voting for that inveterate racist, that George Wallace of the twenty-first century, Hillary Rodham Clinton.

See what I mean? If Democratic primary voters can't get a break from the O-bots, what chance do tea partiers and talk radio listeners have?

Throughout American history, expressing support for values like individual responsibility, personal liberty, and economic freedom was about as radical as choosing pumpkin pie as your favorite Thanksgiving dessert. Until now. Today, it makes you part of the extremist rabble.

And opposing government policy through protests and marches has always been quintessentially American. But in the Obama era, it raises questions about your loyalty, your decency, even your sanity.

That's how my mother became a member of the so-called "angry mob." She's a typical American supporting traditional American values against a government and media elite that oppose them.

That makes her—along with the rest of the tea party, talk radio, and tax protest movement—Government Enemy Number One.

Chapter Four

Honk If I'm Paying Your Mortgage

ike so many sordid tales in my life, it all started with a woman. Her name was Melonie Griffiths-Evans. And she taught me the ways of "hope and change."

Melonie—a poor, unmarried mother of three who worked part-time—somehow got a bank to loan her $470,000 to buy a house in Boston. After two years, she was "shocked" when some sort of adjustable rate thing kicked in. Unable to afford the new payments, she stopped making them. Now she was being forced out of her home by a greedy bank, and she wanted to know what we were going to do about it.

"We" as in "you and me."

It wasn't her fault, she insisted. How was she supposed to know that "adjustable" rates were the kind that *adjust*? Was it fair to expect this simple, good-hearted woman to understand complex financial concepts like "when you borrow $470,000, at some point you have to pay it back?"

No! All she knew was that this was her house, and the bank had no right to take it. She was mad! And she wasn't alone. When I discovered Melonie, she was protesting in the streets outside her home along with a group of "community organizers" and "fair housing advocates"—phrases only vaguely familiar to me at the time.

As the TV cameras rolled, the protestors decried the injustice done to Ms. Griffiths-Evans. Was she really going to lose her home just because she'd spent the past two years *not* paying for it?

Some chanted and marched. Others chained themselves to her front porch (or, to be accurate, to the bank's front porch). Members of a group calling itself "Dorchester People for Peace"— apparently unfamiliar with their own name—threatened violence if Melonie were evicted. "We're bailing out Wall Street," Melonie told the local media. "We ought to be bailing out people like me." Melonie Griffiths-Evans claimed she was a dupe. She was a victim.

Oh, and did I mention she's also a *licensed real estate agent?*

In fact, according to media reports, she had been involved in twenty or so real estate transactions in recent years. So one wonders how many of her own clients ended up complaining they got hosed by one of those same adjustable-rate thingies. But if they did, they'd know who to blame.

Why the bank, of course!

I don't like seeing anyone thrown out of their house, but I really didn't understand how this was the bank's fault. So I asked Melonie about it when she called in to my radio show. Did she

really believe she had the right to stay in a house she wasn't paying for? That her fellow taxpayers were obligated to pay her
mortgage? That it was someone else's duty, and not her own, to
make sure she had a place to live?

Melonie's answers: yes, yes, and yes!

I was genuinely taken aback. How could someone have a
worldview that was the polar opposite of my own when we both
had so much in common?

For example, Melonie told me she always wanted to own her
own house. You know what, Melonie—me, too! Due to my odd
career path, I'd spent most of my adult life as a reluctant renter.

Then she told me it was tough finding a house big enough for
her three kids. "Preach it, Sister," I replied. I have *four* kids, and
I moved to Massachusetts at the peak of the housing bubble when
prices were ridiculous. Growing up in South Carolina, $500,000
could buy you a mansion. In Massachusetts, it got you a dump-
ster with cable. In fact, to get a house large enough for my family, I had taken out a subprime loan—just like Melonie.

But then the market changed, Melonie pointed out. Home values started collapsing, and she couldn't refinance or borrow
against equity or sell for a quick profit. "What's the government
going to do about it?" she demanded.

Hear, hear! The same thing happened to me, so I know how
you...What? Wait a minute. What's the *government* going to do
about it? Well, I assume it's going to do the same thing about your
home value dropping by 20 percent that it did when it was jumping by 20 percent a year—nothing. And you weren't complaining
about government inaction then, were you?

She didn't want to hear it. She had a house. She had a loan.
Somebody, Melonie insisted, was going to take care of this
problem—and it wasn't going to be her. She wasn't picky about

who it would be; the bank could give her a free house, or the tax-payers could buy her one, or some passing alien spacecraft on its way to pick up Louis Farrakahn for a family reunion could beam down a doublewide. But somebody, somewhere, was going to bail her out of this mess.

The whole conversation was surreal. This woman was—on paper, anyway—a real estate professional, and she wanted me and her fellow taxpayers to pay her mortgage. She didn't just expect it—she *demanded* it. And when I argued that she should pay her own bills just like I pay mine, she became outraged.

Suddenly I was the bad guy for suggesting that people should be responsible for the consequences of their own actions. The conversation transformed from "What kind of dope borrows half a million dollars with no way to pay it back?" into "What sort of evil person expects her to?"

Was I some kind of bigot? A hatemonger? Some kind of mean-spirited freak?

When the interview ended, Melonie Griffiths-Evans was absolutely confident she was the hero of this story, and I was the villain. Not long afterward, America elected Barack Obama, and one of his supporters, Peggy Johnson of Sarasota, Florida, rap-turously declared, "I never thought this day would ever happen. I won't have to worry about putting gas in my car. I won't have to worry about paying my mortgage. You know, if I help him, he's going to help me."

I immediately thought of Melonie. She came to mind again a few months later, when a Boston woman moved into an empty three-story townhouse and claimed the "moral right" to live there. She was supported by a "housing rights" group called City Life, which organized round-the-clock squatters to stay in the home and make sure the bank that owned it didn't claim its property.

"People are suffering terribly out there," said Steve Meacham, a prominent liberal activist who helped organize the home invasion. "If these actions can help resolve these situations, they are justified."

Justified. Moral. This is why I prefer an honest thief over a "housing advocate" or a "community organizer." A mugger pulls his gun and takes your money, sure. But he doesn't waste your time arguing he's doing the right thing.

Let's Hope They Don't Blame Themselves

Nothing drives working, bill-paying Americans crazier than the idea that their tax dollars are going to subsidize the bad behavior of others—particularly those who jumped on the housing bubble bandwagon. Whether it's Morgan Stanley or Melonie Griffiths-Evans, typical Americans like my mom are sick of picking up the tab for the greed or bad judgment of others.

Unfortunately, a frightening number of Americans have the "Who's going to pay my bills?" mentality. And that's precisely what the Obama elites are counting on: that the Peggy Johnsons and Melonie Griffiths-Evans of the world will do something for them— vote—and in return the O-bots will do something for them—use our money to pay their bills.

The obstacle to that arrangement is the traditional American notion of individual responsibility. That "rugged individualism" Americans are known for abroad is a real stumbling block for the HopeyChangey crowd here at home. It's hard to create a nationalized, single-payer health system, for example, when citizens

Love Letter from the Left

"What we're seeing right now is close to Brown Shirt tactics. I mean that very seriously."

—Democratic congressman Brian Baird, on townhall protestors

keep insisting they want to buy their own insurance and expect their neighbors to as well.

This is the fundamental ethos of the tea party movement: responsibility. And it is the Kryptonite of Super Obama's belief system. How can he and his big government allies save us from the challenges of life if we keep insisting on saving ourselves?

And so the Obama elites—particularly media liberals—have maintained a steady assault against the notion that individual responsibility is morally superior to collective action. If it bothers you to pay other people's bills, there's something suspect about you. That's Team Obama's message, and they're not trying to hide it, either.

It's certainly not being hidden by Bruce Marks—he's probably the premiere "housing rights" activist in America, and he's definitely the self-described "bank terrorist" most likely to get invited to the White House.

Marks and his ACORN-affiliated group Neighborhood Assistance Corp. of America want to "change how lending is done in America." You see, Marks is angry that there are different types of loans and interest rates for different borrowers, based on their individual behavior. Why should a couple who've been sacrificing for years to save up a down payment be treated differently from a couple who've been blowing their savings every year in Vegas? Is that fair?

Marks doesn't think so. The *Wall Street Journal* reported, "Instead of relying on credit scores, he thinks lenders should look into the reasons for any late payments in prospective borrowers' past and prepare renters for the responsibilities of home ownership. Then, if people are given a loan they can afford, they shouldn't be required to make a down payment, he argues."

Credit scores, schmedit scores. So what if you were slapping trips to Cozumel on the credit card while your neighbor was socking away the savings. Is it fair that he gets a lower interest rate than you? Why should it matter if you've missed a bunch of monthly payments while your neighbor has worked a second job to make sure he didn't? How bogus is that, dude?

Sadly, this is Bruce Marks's argument. And powerful people take him seriously. They have to, because Marks's "terrorist" tactics include organizing pickets of elementary schools where uncooperative bankers send their children. He also clubs bankers into submission by publicizing personal information like their divorce records.

But the greatest evil, Marks realizes, exists not among bankers, but among the American people overall. It's our misguided sense of responsibility.

Marks points to a tragic 2008 case involving a Massachusetts mother. On the day a bank was slated to foreclose on her house and sell it at auction, she wrote the bank a message declaring that, by the time it sold the house, she would be dead. After faxing the message, she committed suicide. It truly was a truly disturbing case.

It was also far more complicated than was generally reported in the local media, which framed the story as a middle-class mother driven over the edge by shame when she was confronted, for the first time, with economic adversity.

In fact, her husband had filed for bankruptcy three times in the previous five years. And the home had actually jumped in value by $100,000, but that money was effectively wiped out because they had borrowed against the equity. There were also seldom-reported personal issues involved, including indications the wife had hidden the foreclosure from her husband. Far from "Middle Class Mom Shamed Into Suicide," this was the case of people who were well aware of their financially risky behavior.

But the facts didn't stop Bruce Marks. He had a point to make, and he was going to make it. "What gets us so angry is that people blame themselves," he told the *Boston Globe*. "They can't see past their sense of responsibility and the predatory nature of these lenders. Unless something more dramatic happens, there's going to be more and more people like her."

Think for a moment about the notion of getting past your "sense of responsibility." Leftist activists are promoting the abandonment of responsibility as a good thing in itself. Worse, they're portraying personal responsibility as a source of danger.

So hard-working, responsible Americans are being driven to suicide by their over-inflated sense of responsibility? If only they'd let someone in government—oh, I dunno, maybe a former junior senator from Illinois, for example—give them billions of other people's money before these excessively responsible folks do something rash.

Marks isn't alone. Liberal academic Brent White of the University of Arizona published research in 2009 arguing that millions of upside-down homeowners "should be walking away in droves." They "have no reasonable prospect of recouping" what they owe on the house, and they're only keeping their mortgage obligations because of an "emotional" sense of personal responsibility.

This is economically irrational, insists White. What they should do is run out and buy everything they can on credit—including, if possible, a mortgage on another house!—then default on their loans and give their bank the brush off. This, White says, will let American borrowers abandon their mortgage obligations "with minimal disruptions to their lifestyles."

And what could possibly be more important than maintaining one's lifestyle? Certainly not maintaining one's integrity, credibility, or self respect. That's only for chumps.

Let me stop the bus right here and ask you this: in your entire adult life, have you ever thought that America had a problem caused by *too much personal responsibility*? Have you ever ·thought, even fleetingly, "Man, people just have to get over this sense that they're responsible for what they do"?

Oh, what a wonderful problem to have.

Instead, we've got obese people who buy Big Macs by the sackful, then sue McDonalds for serving them. We've got lifelong smokers who blame tobacco companies when they get sick. After the slaughter at Fort Hood by Nidal Hasan, reporters even invented a new mental condition—*pre*-traumatic stress disorder—to remove any responsibility from the murderer himself.

Americans feel too much personal responsibility? Why not accuse the French of being too polite to foreigners, or the Canadians of being too much fun at parties?

Such is the worldview of the Obama elites. Now, they're not foolish enough to say straight out, "You shouldn't pay your mortgage." Instead, they'll say, "It's not that big a deal if you don't." And, of course, their most pressing message is this: "Anyone who makes you feel bad for not paying your bills is a rightwing bigot."

The fact is, a disturbing number of Americans have already followed Bruce Marks's advice and "gotten over" that whole personal responsibility thing. In housing, it's so widespread that the real estate industry coined a phrase for it: "jingle mail." Just mail in your keys and abandon your commitments.

The reaction from Washington has been to take hundreds of billions of dollars from taxpayers who *do* pay their bills and give it to people who *don't*. While I have no problem giving a little help to responsible people who've hit a rough patch in the current recession, a lot of this money is going to people who bought houses they knew they could never afford or had no intention of paying for.

Here's one example: a Washington, D.C., area bus driver, Minta Garcia, borrowed $800,000 for a house. According to CNN's Jim Acosta, "Like countless other Americans, Garcia admits she and her husband bought more house than they could afford, but she says the lender made the purchase all too easy. Now her mortgage is worth more than her house."

Yes, curses on that evil mortgage company for lending Garcia the money she asked for. How do they sleep at night? And here's a good question: since Garcia admits she bought more home than she could afford, does she realize that the bank is entitled to take the house back? Not quite.

> **Acosta** (voice-over): Her message to the president…
> **Garcia:** Stop with the foreclosure.
> **Acosta** (on camera): Stop the foreclosures?
> **Garcia:** Yes. Right now, because if people are losing houses, losing jobs, what are we going to do?

Perhaps someone should explain to Garcia that the president isn't foreclosing on anyone. It's not the government at all. It's the bank. And the bank is foreclosing to try to limit the damage Garcia has already done. The bank is going to lose money, leaving it with less money to lend to other people who want to buy a house.

And her solution is to keep the house, so the bank loses even more money? It sounds like Garcia has gotten over her sense of responsibility to me.

According to CNN, Garcia was getting help from President Obama's $75 billion bailout program. And what are that program's results? Most estimates are that 30 percent of those bailed out by taxpayers end up defaulting, anyway—about ten times the rate of default among typical homeowners. In other words, this mortgage plan disproportionately rewards those who've already shown their willingness to walk away from their responsibilities.

Bailout Nation

Bailouts—whether they're for AIG or Minta Garcia—drive normal Americans bonkers. They're one of the primary instigators of tea parties. It's not because our fellow Americans are being given something. As I already said, we're the most charitable nation on earth.

No, it's because the bailout regime that began under President Bush and blossomed under Obama has repeatedly rewarded those who engaged in bad behavior—and the worse the behavior, the bigger the bailout. The people left holding the bag are those who've sacrificed immediate gratification to do the right thing. They were dumping their change every night into a blue water bottle in the closet of their dumpy apartment, saving for a down payment on their future dream home. Meanwhile, their neighbor was moving into a house he couldn't afford, on a no-money-down, interest-only subprime loan backed by Freddie and Fannie, hoping to ride the real estate bubble and flip it at a profit.

When the bubble burst, who got taken care of? Not the responsible saver—he'd love to buy up that house at the new, low price.

But instead, President Obama and Congress took his tax money and used it to keep the speculator in the house, artificially inflating the price of all real estate along the way.

Not only did responsible "Regular Guy" get screwed—he got screwed with his own money! And it went to Billy Joe Bailout, who's happy to give Obama credit for saving "his" home.

Having helped organize tea parties and other taxpayer protest events, I saw first hand that opposition to bailouts was one of the primary reasons why more than one million Americans took to the streets on a busy workday in April 2009 to send a message to their government.

Don't take my word for it. Just read some of the most popular signs: "You keep your bailout, I'll keep my freedom," "Congress is a toxic asset," and the classic, "Dude, where's MY bailout?"

But the crowds that thronged American cities from coast to coast that day weren't really looking for bailouts. These moms and dads, small business owners and union members, self-employed and retired workers, young and old Americans—they were just trying to tell Washington and the American political class one thing: "Enough!"

We don't want to be bailed out, bribed, or babied. We want a nation of independent citizens who stand on their own two feet, in good times and in bad. We want this country to value responsibility and sacrifice, not bailouts and giveaways. This isn't a question of economics—or the questionable economics of the Obama administration. For typical Americans, this is a question of character.

But the mainstream media refuses to understand that. The most glaring example was seen at the April 15 Chicago tea party, where CNN "reporter" Susan Roesgen, impersonating an angry MoveOn.org member, demanded to know why the protestors refused to be bribed by tax credits or stimulus funds:

Susan Roesgen: [reading signs held by protesters] Uh, let's see…"Drop the taxes," "Drop socialism." [speaking to protestor and reading his sign] Okay, let's see, you're here with your two-year-old and you're already in debt. Why are you here today, sir?

Man: Because I heard a president say that he believed in what Lincoln stood for. Lincoln's primary thing was he believed that people had the right to liberty, and had the right…

Roesgen: Sir, what does this have to do with taxes? What does this have to do with your taxes? Do you realize that you're eligible for a $400 credit…

Man: Let me finish my point. Lincoln, Lincoln believed that people had the right to share in the fruits of their own labor and that government should not take it. And we have clearly gotten to that point.

Roesgen: Wait, wait. Did you know that the state of Lincoln gets $50 billion out of the stimulus? That's $50 billion for this state, sir.

Man: Ma'am, ma'am, ma'am, I…I…I…

Roesgen: Okay, well, Kyra, we'll move on over here. I think you get the general tenor of this. Uh, it's anti-government, anti-CNN, since this is highly promoted by the rightwing conservative network, FOX. And since I can't really hear much more, and I think this is not really family viewing. Toss it back to you, Kyra.

Roesgen was right. FOX News is very different from CNN. For one thing, I've never seen a FOX field reporter shout down an interview subject.

Roesgen and the rest of the mainstream media couldn't comprehend that the protesters weren't just talking about money.

They weren't looking for a $400 handout of their own tax dollars, and they understood that the $50 billion in "free" money was debt that would have to be paid back by the 2-year-old.

The protestors were making the case that it was wrong—morally and ethically wrong—to throw $13 trillion in debt on the backs of future generations, particularly so you could give the money to the Melonie Griffiths-Evans, AIGs, and CitiGroups of today. Even if these deadbeats deserved the money—and they don't—shafting our kids to do it is unacceptable.

And so the tea partiers sent a message: we're fighting back. We're done rewarding bad behavior and punishing the responsible. We're finished beating down taxpayers to keep the government sector fat and happy. We're sick and tired of watching well-connected fat cats rolling in our taxpayer dough.

It would be one thing if we were all in this together. But we're not. The "spread the wealth" philosophy is an open declaration that some people are going to be declared winners (getting bailouts) and others losers (paying bailouts).

Interestingly, the likelihood of being declared a winner in the new Bailout Nation is directly correlated to the likelihood that you're a loser in real life. Did you make irresponsible and irrational decisions? Blow off your house payments? Drop out of school? Make risky investments with other people's money? Ruin your company by loaning lots of cash to deadbeats with no income?

Congratulations, you WIN!

On the other hand, are you one of those tragic Americans who can't get over your sense of personal responsibility, who spent only what you could afford, and didn't max out your home equity to pay for weekend trips to the Bunny Ranch? Do you still insist on doing your own math instead of swallowing the numbers fed to you by the mainstream media? Are you one of those "cynics" who

refuse to believe the
Easter Bunny is going
to leave $11 trillion
under President Obama's
pillow? Do you cling to the
delusion that the great American experiment will fail if we
reject its two key ingredients:
responsibility and accountability?

In that case, the Congressional Budget Office has a
new term for you: "sucker."

The typical Americans
who make up the tea partiers
are the suckers—and we
know it. The tea party movement rose up on behalf of all the
bill-paying, mortgage-making, tax-paying, hard-working, family-
protecting, neighborhood-watching, America-loving everyday
citizens who still believe that the American Dream cannot be
built on debt, hope, and spare change.

Good people make good government. But government cannot
make good people. They can only make irresponsible people *feel*
good, usually at their neighbor's expense.

> ## Love Letter from the Left
>
> "Much will depend on just how cynical those encouraging the mob frenzy are—while denying responsibility. What shall we call them? Mobsters?"
>
> —former CNN reporter Bob Franken, on conservative leaders who are supposedly inciting tea partiers

Extreme Rake-Over: Taxpayers' Edition

Personal responsibility has become so unpopular you can't give it
away.

In 2005, Patricia and Milton Harper of Clayton County, Georgia, were handed the keys to their brand-new, four-bedroom

dream home by Ty Pennington of ABC's *Extreme Makeover*. And "dream" is the right word. The Harpers' new home included four fireplaces, a music room with eight turntables, and a solarium. At the time it was the largest *Extreme Makeover* project ever undertaken, involving some 1,800 volunteers.

Not only that, but the Beazer Home professionals who donated their labor also chipped in another $250,000 to help cover college tuition for the Harpers' three sons as well as the couple's property taxes and maintenance for years to come. And it all happened on national TV before an audience of millions.

Three years later, the Harpers stood before a much smaller audience and watched as their home was sold at auction on the Clayton County courthouse steps.

A free house, a sack of dough, and the Harpers still managed to lose it all. How? First, they borrowed $450,000 against the house's equity and blew it on a risky business venture. Then they stopped paying it back. The Harpers declined to talk to the media about their downfall, but one neighbor delicately explained, "They were never good with money."

You've probably known people like that. We've all certainly been around people like that. To be honest, for a large part of my misspent youth *I* was like that. But I don't remember asking for a bailout from anyone other than my put-upon parents.

If only the Harpers had held on another year until the Obama stimulus plan, they might have gotten a TV-Show-Winners-Who-Were-Still-Too-Clueless-to-Keep-the-House bailout.

I hope everything works out for the Harper family. But their story shows the violence that the "spread the wealth" bailout culture does to the core values of typical Americans. The mayor of Lake City, Georgia, who worked on the Harpers' house himself, said it all: "It's aggravating. It just makes you mad. You do that much work, and they just squander it."

But everyday Americans know that people who get things for free tend to squander them. Not always, and not because they're lazy bums who've never tried to succeed. But when you're using other people's money or you know a bailout is on the way, there's a big temptation to do irresponsible things you wouldn't normally do.

How are the Harpers any different from the bankers and mortgage brokers who revved up the housing bubble that eventually crashed the markets in 2008? Do you ever wonder how people like our friend Melonie Griffiths-Evans got these massive loans in the first place?

It's because Congressional liberals like Congressman Barney Frank and Senator Chris Dodd pushed for government policies to pressure banks to make these loans. They explicitly warned lenders to judge loan applicants not based on their ability to repay, but rather on their demographic status as low-income and minority borrowers (and their corresponding political status as likely liberal voters).

The trail to oblivion was blazed by semi-government lending giants Fannie Mae and Freddie Mac. As George Mason University economist Russell Roberts reports, "For 1996, the Department of Housing and Urban Development (HUD) gave Fannie and Freddie an explicit target—42% of their mortgage financing had to go to borrowers with income below the median in their area. The target increased to 50% in 2000 and 52% in 2005."

In the *Wall Street Journal*, Roberts further noted,

> For 1996, HUD required that 12% of all mortgage purchases by Fannie and Freddie be "special affordable" loans, typically to borrowers with income less than 60% of their area's median income. That number was increased to 20% in 2000 and 22% in 2005. The 2008 goal was to be 28%.

Between 2000 and 2005, Fannie and Freddie met those goals every year, funding hundreds of billions of dollars worth of loans, many of them subprime and adjustable-rate loans, and made to borrowers who bought houses with less than 10% down.

Unsurprisingly, people who needed "special affordable" (read: "subprime") loans tended to be risky borrowers—and once again, in full disclosure, I was one of them.

But with the government ordering these loans to be made, and with Fannie and Freddie buying up billions of subprime securities themselves, the net result was that riskier borrowers became preferred borrowers. Regular would-be homeowners were actually at a disadvantage, while folks like the Harpers were on the fast track.

This upside-down accountability is so ingrained in our governing class that liberals like Barney Frank were still pushing for non-market-based lending in late 2009—after the effects of their disaster had sunk the whole economy.

And once again, the good guys somehow get turned into the bad guys. Take Joe Petrucelli of East Bridgewater Savings Bank. In late 2008, when many bankers were looking for a tall building with a short ledge, East Bridgewater had no delinquent loans and no homes in foreclosure. It even turned a small profit in the last quarter of the year. Joe Petrucelli didn't take a single bailout dime. He didn't need it. And what did he get for his trouble?

His bank was cited by banking regulators for being too cautious in its lending. Where were the subprime loans and the aggressive marketing of riskier loan products? Not at East Bridgewater, which is one reason the bank was in such good shape—or bad shape, as Barney Frank sees it.

A banker does everything right, and he's a problem. The government continues to push banks to make the very kinds of loans that started the economic avalanche, and the O-bots still claim more government bailouts are the solution. Meanwhile, liberal activists tell irresponsible borrowers to blame the banks instead of themselves.

America, is it getting crazy in here, or is it just me?

Chapter Five

PAGING DR. HOUSE

I love the TV show *House*. I don't usually like doctor shows, and I have to close my eyes when the camera zooms into the icky bits of the human anatomy. But *House* is great because of its main character, Dr. Gregory House, played superbly by British actor Hugh Laurie.

Not to put too fine a point on it, but House is a total a-hole. Rude, selfish, condescending—he treats his peers like dirt and his patients even worse. And we love it! Why? In part because he's willing to acknowledge his own flaws and failings. In part because he's witty and fun to watch. But mostly because he's absolutely brilliant. Dr. House is almost always right.

When you're Dr. Greg House, you're so smart you can get away with demeaning the intellect of everyone else. And that rings true in real life. We've all had teachers, coaches, or bosses who were rude, condescending jerks, but who got away with it because, unfortunately, they were usually right.

So having my intellect insulted by someone like Greg House, I could handle. But getting called stupid by...*Joe Biden?*

That's where I draw the line.

During his failed 1988 presidential campaign, Biden famously commented on his own intelligence. The exchange happened at a coffee klatch in New Hampshire, after a voter asked Biden where he attended law school and what degrees he had. Offended that a mere peasant dare challenge the intellect of a Great and Powerful Liberal, Biden offered up this classic response:

> I think I probably have a much higher IQ than you do, I suspect. I went to law school on a full academic scholarship—the only one in my class to have a full academic scholarship....I won the international moot court competition. I was the outstanding student in the political science department at the end of my year. I graduated with three degrees from undergraduate school, and 165 credits—only needed 123—and I'd be delighted to sit down and compare my IQ to yours.

Our future vice president certainly put that upstart citizen in his place. Or he would have, if anything he said had actually been true.

As the *New York Times* reported, Biden did not get a "full academic scholarship," nor did he graduate at the top of his class—unless you're doing politically correct math and all the children are above average. Joe the Genius actually graduated seventy-sixth in his class at prestigious Syracuse Law School (koff, koff). Out of a class of eighty-five.

(What do you call a guy who graduates in last place from med school? "Doctor." From law school? "Mr. Vice President.")

As an undergrad, Biden was never named "outstanding student" by the political science department at the University of Delaware. There is no proof he "won the international moot court competition," though he competed in a regular moot court event in Canada in 1967. And as for the "three degrees from undergraduate school," the *Times* reported stoically, "Mr. Biden received a single B.A. in history and political science."

Dr. House, he's not. No, Joe Biden's more of a Maxwell Smart: "Missed it by THAT much!"

Now, it's not completely fair to indict the intellect of the entire American liberal establishment over Joe Biden. Indeed, his gaseous gaffery transcends politics, partisanship, and perhaps even time and space.

Listening to Biden speak ("It happens to be, as Barack says, a three letter word: Jobs. J-O-B-S"), his arrogant absence-of-all-clueness is so profound that I sometimes wonder if there isn't a parallel universe in another dimension where his insanity makes sense. Really, I think there are probably aliens out there somewhere that would appreciate some of Biden's classic statements, like this one: "A man I'm proud to call my friend. A man who will be the next president of the United States—Barack America!" If only we could find the right wormhole to put him through, Biden could return to his native planet and become the great leader he thinks he already is.

Though perhaps not as great as FDR who, according to Biden, "when the stock market crashed...got on the television and didn't just talk about the princes of greed."

Gee, Mr. Vice President, what exactly *did* Roosevelt talk about in his 1929 TV broadcasts? Was it that hilarious moment when

President Hoover showed up in the Oval Office and said, "Franklin, what the hell are you doing in here? You won't be elected until 1932, you idiot! And what are you doing on commercial television? Don't you know it hasn't been invented yet?"

Then again, what do I know? I'm just one of those bitter, clingy, tea party types. I listen to talk radio, read the editorial page of the *Wall Street Journal* and watch FOX News. Why, I even friended Sarah Palin on Facebook. All of which makes me intellectually suspect—among liberals, anyway.

If you're a normal person, you've probably experienced it firsthand. Some co-workers or cocktail party attendees are spouting the approved liberal agit-prop about whatever—global warming, terrorism, healthcare, the college football BCS system—and you voice a contrary opinion. Suspicions are suddenly aroused, and the O-bots turn on you.

You're told, "You can't be serious," or "I bet you listen to Rush Limbaugh," or in one case I'm familiar with, a guy who questioned the wisdom of spending billions to fight global warming was informed, "You can't be THAT stupid."

Do you, my Lefty American friends, have any idea what it's like being called stupid by people who voted for Jimmy Carter, John Edwards, and—in some extreme cases—Howard Dean and Al Sharpton? Are you kidding me?

And once again, you hardly ever hear everyday conservatives insult liberals like this, primarily because typical Americans aren't that arrogant about their opinions. Obviously I'm generalizing, but normal people are raised to at least listen to other viewpoints and show some basic level of tolerance. They rarely resort to the standard liberal method of argument: call someone an idiot and then dismiss him without a hearing. Normal Americans just aren't that rude. Unlike the O-bots, we actually believe in the only form of diversity with real value: diversity of thought.

Now, I am not in the "there's no such thing as a stupid question" camp at all. There are plenty of stupid questions, and plenty of nitwits of all political stripes asking them. (If you're still asking to see Obama's birth certificate, for example, you shouldn't have made it this far into the book.) I see no reason to humor the egregiously stupid.

So, for example, when callers to my show want to debate the proposition that my opinions are fed to me via fax from my Zionist masters at the Illuminati Division of Bilderberg's World Headquarters, I just end the conversation.

Not many people think anyone's obligated to debate a kook, but legitimate questions deserve answers, especially when they're directed at our supposed public servants. A guy shows up at a townhall meeting and asks, "Hey—who's gonna pay for all this 'free' healthcare?" It's a completely legitimate question, one that as of this writing still hasn't been answered. But the media treat the questioner like some bonehead who's quoting from the Cliffs-Notes edition of the *Protocols of the Elders of Zion*.

And it's even more grating when those attacks on our intellect come from people with the intellectual heft of, say, DNC chair Howard Dean—a man who, when a reporter asked for his favorite book in the New Testament, replied "Job."

Well, at least he knew it was a three-letter word.

Or consider Senator Harry Reid, who denied we have a compulsory income tax system. ("In fact quite the contrary, our system of governing is a voluntary tax system.") Or House Judiciary chairman John Conyers, who admitted he doesn't read or understand legislation he votes on. ("What good is reading the bill if it's a thousand pages and you don't have two days and two lawyers to find out what it means after you read the bill?")

Then there's the *New York Times*, claiming Dan Rather's bogus story on Bush's Air National Guard service was "fake, but accurate." Or Dan Rather himself, who even after Monicagate was fully exposed, said of Bill Clinton, "I think he's an honest man....I think you can be an honest person and lie about any number of things."

Not to mention Michael Moore ("There is no terrorist threat"), Rosie O'Donnell ("Radical Christianity is just as threatening as radical Islam in a country like America"), and on and on.

I know what you're thinking, my liberal friends: no matter how many examples of idiocy there are by prominent liberals across the fifty-seven states of Obama's America, in your heart you still know liberals are smarter than everyone else.

The arrogance of assumed superiority is there in President Obama's painfully condescending depiction of Americans as "confused" but "basically decent." It's there in liberal Ted Turner's comment that "the United States has some of the dumbest people in the world." It was there in the liberals' reaction to President Bush's 2004 reelection; Slate.com ran an article by liberal novelist Jane Smiley bemoaning "the Unteachable Ignorance of the Red States"—a sentiment echoed abroad on a front page headline of Britain's *Daily Mirror*, which asked, "How can 59,054,087 people be so DUMB?"

But the greatest insult of all is the belief of the Obama elites that the American people can't be trusted to manage their own healthcare, raise their own children, or run their own businesses. It's not that the O-bots *want* to run the country for the rest of us, you see, it's that they *must*, because we're just too stupid to do it ourselves This is one of the primal fantasies fed by the ideological identity politics of Barack "Harvard Law Review" Obama.

What makes liberals think they're smarter than their fellow Americans? Do they base their views on any empirical data? (For

Keith Olbermann fans, that means "things you can measure and stuff like that to prove your point.")

Well, statistics *are* available on this, but I can understand why liberals don't like to talk about them. For example, a 2006 Pew Research study found that talk radio listeners in general—and Rush Limbaugh listeners in particular—are more knowledgeable about current events and have more education than the audiences of CNN, MSNBC, *Meet the Press*, or other liberal venues. In fact, Limbaugh's audience ranked only behind readers of the *Weekly Standard* and the *New Republic* in general knowledge.

Talk radio listeners are also better educated and better informed than readers of daily papers like the *New York Times* or *Washington Post*. That's no surprise, since talk radio covers stories the mainstream media won't, like progress in Iraq, Obama's lunatic policy czars, and global warming scandals. As Randall Bloomquist, a longtime radio journalist and programmer, noted, "The talk radio audience is *not* representative of America—it's better educated, more affluent, and more mature than the nation as a whole. Roughly three-quarters of talk listeners have at least some college. Nearly 50% make more than $75,000 a year."

Even liberal academic and communications expert Dr. Kathleen Hall Jamieson, a frequent critic of conservative media, describes talk listeners as "politically interested. They're high consumers of media, including high consumers of mainstream media. And they're much more likely to be politically active. That is, write letters, make phone calls, and participate in the political process by voting."

There's more: in 2008, *Psychology Today* reported on a series of studies by sociologist Markus Kemmelmeier, comparing self-declared ideology and college entrance exam results. Kemmelmeier admitted he expected liberal views would correlate to higher ability levels, but instead the results were mixed: while social conservatives had lower test scores, economic/libertarian-leaning conservatives aced their liberal counterparts.

Kemmelmeier then looked at high school test results and voting patterns at the state level. Again, results were mixed. His previous assumptions of liberal primacy "would be very wrong—at least as a general conclusion," Kemmelmeier reported.

Yes, it's true that people with advanced degrees tend to vote Left. But it's also true that people smart enough actually to *do* stuff—brilliant business professionals, for example—tend to vote Right.

And as for the "college degree" argument, I'd like to point out that Joe Biden claims to have three of 'em—not to mention being voted "Most Likely to Suffer Brain Damage During Hair Plug Surgery" by his fellow MENSA members—and you see how well that worked out. ("You know, I'm embarrassed—do you know the website number?")

So why the constant disparaging comments from media elites about the intellect of tea party attendees and talk radio listeners? Are there dopes in the tea party movement? Of course. There are dim bulbs on both sides of the marquee. The Left has Thomas Friedman but gets stuck with Michael Moore. The Right has George Will but gets stuck with Michael Graham. Can't we call it even?

The idea that modern conservatism—an ideological group that includes Milton Freidman, Thomas Sowell, Peggy Noonan, and William F. Buckley, Jr.—is the last refuge of the short-bus riders is patently absurd.

And while liberals love to hate them, the fact is that pop-culture conservatives like Rush Limbaugh and Ann Coulter are very smart people. Lefties may use their names to frighten naughty children around nighttime campfires, but these folks aren't dumb. Wrong?

Perhaps. Evil? If Harry Reid says so. But stupid? Obviously not.

Therefore, given the intellectual accomplishments and failures on both sides, we should view the debate over Obamanomics as a legitimate disagreement between two groups that each have valid points to make. That's the "here's why I think I'm right and you're wrong" approach.

But when you actually try to debate an O-bot, what you hear is, "I *know* I'm right, and I think you should get a job playing banjo in dinner theater re-makes of *Deliverance*."

> ## Love Letter from the Left
>
> "As has always happened when progressive change is in the air, the backlash gets fierce, ugly and anti-American.... Let's be clear who we are talking about—call them attack dogs, call them Teabaggers, call them Glenn Beck."
>
> —Andy Stern, President of the Service Employees International Union (SEIU)

Okay, fine. But while Obama and his allies are busy insulting normal people, we're busy noticing that, for the Smartest People in the World, Team Obama can be exceptionally stupid.

It Must Be Liberalism, 'Cuz I Feel So Dumb

Of all the sectors of Americans that might have the credibility to insult the intellect of others, the Left is at or near the bottom. Is there a collection of Americans more clueless than the Obama elites who govern us? If so, where would we find them? Operating carnival rides in Coney Island? Sending their personal bank information to a Nigerian emailer?

In the arena of politics and public policy, Team Obama is the worst possible combination of arrogance and error. Its leaders have the insufferable attitude of Dr. House, but the intellectual credibility of Sonya Fitzpatrick, Animal Psychic. Their "smartest guy in the room" attitude is bad enough, but coming from people who've been wrong about nearly everything, it's utterly unbearable.

And "wrong about nearly everything" isn't the opinion of just one talk show host. It's the demonstrable, measurable track record of modern liberalism. In my adult lifetime, the American Left has been wrong about almost every major issue of the day. And I only say "almost" out of common courtesy. I honestly can't think of anything the Left has gotten right.

The first year I was old enough to vote for president was 1984. Being a typical college punk, I naturally voted against the evil Ronald Reagan, preferring the far superior liberal leadership of that human dynamo, Walter Mondale. It's the dumbest vote I've ever cast—and I voted for George W. Bush *twice*.

Well, I'm sure not going to vote for a lefty again in light of liberalism's track record. Here's a recent example: on the twentieth anniversary of the fall of the Berlin Wall—an event as monumental to human history as V-E Day and V-J Day combined—President Obama had this to say:

[cue crickets]

Nothing. Any normal president would have gone to Berlin to commemorate the historic occasion, but Obama didn't find the anniversary worthy of even a casual remark. And why not? Why wouldn't a Nobel Laureate have something to say about the liberation of 100 million people from tyranny and oppression?

Perhaps because during the 1980s, American liberals like John Kerry and Nancy Pelosi—not to mention campus activists like a young Barack H. Obama—marched in the streets against the "hatemongering" Ronald Reagan. Worse, liberal stalwart Ted Kennedy made a secret offer to Yuri Andropov to help the decrepit Soviet leader oppose Reagan's policies. A sitting U.S. senator reaching out to help the Soviets? Back in 1983, it seemed like the thing to do.

The American Left's foreign policy was—and remains—appeasement. Many of the same liberals who mock the "strategery" of George W. Bush today spent the Reagan era blaming America for the Cold War and arguing that the Soviet Union was our moral equal—if not our superior. If the libs had prevailed, one of the greatest evils of the modern era—Soviet Communism—might still be enslaving millions today.

The average Joe on the street who supported Reagan was right. The elitist liberals who dismissed him as a cowboy?

Wrong.

Then there were Reagan's tax policies. Liberals were horrified by Reagan's "tax cuts for the rich." (Yep, they were using the same lines thirty years ago. You'd think these brilliant lefties could write some new material.) But instead of collapsing the poor, starving government, the tax cuts caused billions in new money to pour into the Treasury and sparked a job-creating expansion that ran virtually uninterrupted until 2009. Even Bill Clinton and a Democrat-controlled Congress left Reagan's tax policy mostly unchanged.

Two of the three greatest policy debates of the past twenty-five years—the Cold War and Reaganomics—and the liberals elites from the *New York Times* to the Democratic Party got them utterly wrong. The voters, however, saw things clearly, giving Reagan ninety-three states out of 100 in his two election campaigns.

Liberals: tell me why I'm supposed to be cowed by your intellect again?

The other major issue of my adult lifetime is terrorism—and I'll concede this one isn't so cut and dry. America's policy toward international terrorism was a bipartisan muddle for years. Until September 11.

That fateful day brought a choice between two different approaches. One was the "treat terrorism as a form of international crime" approach used by the Clinton administration and supported by good leftwing types.

From the first World Trade Center attack in 1993 until September 2001, America sent virtually no troops abroad to fight terror. We essentially sent lawyers. Having found bin Laden, we made some half-hearted attempts to work with other governments to capture him. But when we had him literally in our sights at a hunting lodge in Afghanistan, we caved to concerns about international law and refused to take him out. It was the international equivalent of waiting to get a search warrant. During those eight years, we suffered a major terror attack about every eighteen months, from New York to Saudi Arabia to Africa to Yemen, culminating in September 11.

That's when we tried something new: treating terrorism as a form of warfare. Declaring terrorists "unlawful combatants" rather than the legal equivalent of bank robbers, we hunted them down and subjected terrorism-promoting nations to serious consequences, up to and including regime change. President Bush sent the military to Afghanistan where it quickly toppled al Qaeda's hosts, the Taliban regime.

The people we captured weren't criminals, and they weren't served with warrants. We locked them up in Guantanamo Bay and waterboarded three of them for information about upcoming attacks, a strategy that even President Obama's inspector general and CIA chief later admitted offered up valuable intelligence.

Liberals oppose this approach. They demand that terrorists receive lawyers, that Guantanamo Bay be shut down, and that the Patriot Act be gutted. Demonstrating a strange inversion of priorities, the Obama administration announced in 2009 it will investigate our own CIA interrogators, despite the fact that their efforts almost surely saved lives.

Following September 11, some on the far Left even rejected our right to use force to defend ourselves at all. Immediately after the attack, Columbia history professor Eric Foner declared, "I'm not sure which is more frightening: the horror that engulfed New York City or the apocalyptic rhetoric emanating daily from the White House." According to a CBS poll shortly after September 11, only 60 percent of self-identified liberals supported a military response if it meant civilian casualties.

And of course, President Bush ordered the military to overthrow the Saddam Hussein regime in Iraq, sparking a huge outcry on the Left against American "warmongering."

But after America toppled the Butcher of Bagdad, something strange happened.

Nothing.

No successful terror attacks on American soil or major American targets abroad. Terror sponsoring regimes became terrorist-hunting ones. After years of escalating terrorist attacks against the United States, the policy opposed by the internationalist, "George Bush is a Neanderthal" Left resulted in no attacks on the American homeland. None.

In 2006, we were tested again as the war in Iraq bogged down. What was the solution? Liberals like John Kerry wanted to get out. Liberals like Obama never wanted to go in at all. So when

Bush chose to back General Petraeus's surge strategy, liberals spoke with one voice: it's an unworkable disaster. Predicting failure, then Senator Obama voted against the surge and continued to denounce it even in 2008, after it *had* worked. Democratic Senate leader Harry Reid went even further. "The war is lost," he proclaimed in April 2007, just as the surge was beginning to turn the tide.

So, to review, liberals were wrong on how to fight terror after September 11, and wrong again on Iraq and the surge. Has the Left gotten *anything* right since the Reagan era? Well, they were good on a few issues—they devised a good strategy for confronting South Africa's apartheid government, and they were right on a few free speech issues. But man, did they get a lot of big stuff wrong, even aside from wars, terrorism, and homeland defense. Here is a partial list:

Welfare reform? Completely wrong. At the behest of liberals, President Clinton vetoed welfare reform twice—and would have again if his pollster, Dick Morris, hadn't stopped him. Liberals predicted disaster. But instead of starving mommies appearing in the streets, welfare rolls plunged by about half, unemployment fell sharply among single moms, and people rediscovered the dignity of work.

Stopping the spread of nukes to whackjob regimes? We may have had faulty intelligence about Saddam Hussein's weapons of mass destruction program, but the Iraq War is still the only policy that's helped reverse the spread of WMDs; afraid of ending up like Saddam, Libyan nutjob Moammar Khaddafi gave up his WMD program after seeing U.S. soldiers roll into Bagdad.

Obama has opted for a different approach, and boy, is that whole "reaching out to the Iranians" thing working *great*. The regime almost apologized as it gunned down protesters in the streets of Tehran, and the mullahs looked a bit bashful as they fired up ever more nuclear centrifuges in the face of Obama's opposition. Why, at one point Ahmedinejad looked like he might, for a moment, consider feeling slightly bad about Iran's funding of terror groups like Hezbollah. Just a little bit. It was in his eyes. You had to look really, really close.

Global warming panic? Insisting evil humans are going to fry the earth like an egg any day now, the knee-jerk Left has been demanding for twenty years that we stop debating the science and start slashing carbon emissions. They denounce those who question their apocalyptic warnings as "deniers," implicitly comparing us to neo-Nazis who deny the Holocaust.

But inconvenient facts keep popping up. Global warmists have been forced to admit the earth hasn't warmed since the late 1990s and may not warm for decades more. Even the leftwing greens at the BBC had to run an article asking, "What Happened to Global Warming?"

But the real blow came with the "ClimateGate" email scandal of 2009, when an alleged hacker published more than 1,000 previously secret emails shared among key global-warming scientist/activists. Aside from their plots to suppress the publication of skeptical research, their use of phrases like "hide the decline" and "destroy any emails" offered a glimpse of the politicized, corrupted research underlying the entire global warming panic.

Today, years after first declaring "there is no debate," global warming liberals once again find themselves embroiled in one. And based on the polls as well as massive public opposition to Obama's cap-and-trade scheme, they are losing.

Illegal immigration? Although they've developed an entire dictionary of euphemisms—"earned citizenship," "path to citizenship," "comprehensive reform"—the Left's immigration policy consists of one word: amnesty. Unfortunately, even some conservatives have been taken in by this, as exemplified by President Reagan's signing of a liberal-backed amnesty bill in 1986. The result? A surge in illegal immigration, as the next generation of illegals lined up for their own amnesty lottery ticket.

By 1990, it was clear that amnesty was a mistake. The difference between tea partiers and Team Obama is that, 20 million illegals and billions of lost tax dollars later, we have learned from that mistake. Washington liberals haven't.

Abortion? Okay, this isn't a black-or-white issue, but the liberal premise that abortions should be viewed as morally neutral medical procedures—the "women's health" version of a tonsillectomy—has been eviscerated. Recent polling shows that despite the media's overwhelming pro-abortion activism, a majority of Americans now consider themselves pro-life. Even the Democrat-dominated, Pelosi-led House of Representatives voted to ban taxpayer-funded abortions.

Shut Up, They Explained

You'd think that people who hadn't gotten things right since JFK was in office would show a bit more modesty—less name calling, more willingness to consider different opinions. Instead, we've got liberals who trash talk their politics like a Dallas Cowboy defensive back, despite having a Detroit Lions record of defeats. It's nonstop arrogance, attack, and attitude directed at all dissent.

I debate ideas and policies for a living. And I do it on the radio where, when I'm wrong, it happens in front of a mass audience that is extremely happy to correct me. So while I passionately believe I'm right, I'm also aware that I could be completely nuts on any given topic. Worse, I could be revealed as such live on the air.

And that's why I find the Left's disconnect between its miserable record and its moral certainty so surprising. If I were a mental health professional, I might find it pathological. And it's not getting any better.

Chief among the trash talkers is Congressman Barney Frank. During the healthcare debate he "quipped" (a word the press uses for remarks that are supposed to be jokes but aren't actually funny) that being among tea party protesters was "like being trapped in a furniture warehouse." This echoed an insult he hurled at a constituent during a townhall meeting: "Trying to have a conversation with you would be like trying to argue with a dining room table."

Granted, the target of that second insult was a Lyndon LaRouche kook, but she was also a citizen. Why not just tell her, "I disagree with you," and politely move on to a more sane questioner?

At that same meeting, another attendee reasonably observed that Frank aimed to put more Americans into Medicare or a Medicare-like system even though Medicare is going bankrupt. After insulting the man a few times ("I don't understand your mentality!"), Frank answered with this bit of witty repartee: "Is Medicare bankrupt? No, it's not technically bankrupt. It needs more money."

It's not bankrupt, it just needs more money? That's like saying Barney Frank's former boyfriend, Stephen Gobie, wasn't a gay prostitute, he was just a guy who got paid to have sex with other guys. At Congressman Frank's house. Until he was eventually caught by the police. Really. I'm not kidding. Google it. (Warning: NSFW).

Frank's next boyfriend was Herb Moses, an executive at Fannie Mae during the time when Frank's congressional committee

Love Letter from the Left

"It's incredibly stupid."

—liberal blogger and former *Atlantic Monthly* writer Matthew Yglesias, on the early tea party movement

oversaw the company. Frank kept the money flowing to Fannie and repeatedly opposed new regulations to slow its risky mortgage activity. The result was hundreds of millions of taxpayer dollars to bail out the devastated company.

And have you met Congressman Frank's newest boyfriend, James Ready? Frank was at his house in Maine in 2005 when Ready was busted for growing pot right on the property. Lots of it. Ready was charged with possession and cultivation. Congressman Frank, a frequent guest, denied knowing anything about the pot, or his boyfriend's repeated use of it, or, well, anything related to agriculture whatsoever.

"I'm not good at plants," Frank said. "I would not recognize marijuana right now if I saw it.... I am not a great outdoorsman." I don't know about you, but I score all my pot from Paul Bunyan.

This is all from the Democrats' number one, smartest, and most powerful congressman. Oh, and he thinks *you're* the dumb one.

Another candidate for the "What's Your Congressman Smoking?" Club is Maxine Waters. She, too, has a dim view of citizen protesters. "I want those people talked to; I want them interviewed," Waters told liberal radio host Bill Press after the mammoth Washington, D.C., tea party on September 12, 2009. "I want journalists to be all over those rallies and the marches with the Birthers and the teabaggers."

At least she doesn't reserve her insults just for us little people; Waters also called senators who don't support ObamaCare "Neanderthals."

Actually "Neanderthal" would be an evolutionary promotion for the California congresswoman. This is a person who wants the government to take over and run, not just the healthcare system, but every American oil company, too. With apologies to Geico, even a caveman knows that's stupid. Did she miss the entire history of Soviet communism?

So steeped in wild-eyed irrationality is Ms. Waters that, when she was interrogating members of the banking industry after the 2008 market meltdown, it was (in the memorable words of the *Atlantic*'s Megan McArdle) "like watching your crazy aunt challenge your boyfriend to prove that fairies aren't real."

Then there are her brilliant insights as an urban sociologist. After Los Angeles rioters trashed their own neighborhoods, looted and torched hundreds of stores, and beat, robbed, and killed passers-by, Waters insisted, "The riots are the voice of the unheard."

So Maxine wants you investigated for showing up at a rally with a "Taxed Enough Already" sign, but an actual "set the liquor stores on fire" riot is just a form of speech? And get this: not long after defending the rioters, *ABC News* named her their "Person of the Week" for her work on urban policy.

Seriously. That's not a joke. Well, at least not an intentional one.

Then there's "supersmart" Tim Geithner, the Treasury Secretary who claimed not to realize that, when you file to be reimbursed for taxes paid, you're supposed to have actually *paid* your taxes.

And don't forget genius congressman Charlie Rangel who, upon seeing millions of American tea partiers protest irresponsible government spending, came to the brilliant conclusion that they're all racists, and that "some Americans have not gotten over the fact that Obama is president." Meanwhile, Rangel forgot to report rental income on one of his properties for *eight consecutive years*. He also "miscalculated" his worth on his disclosure and tax documents by more than 100 percent after forgetting some of his property even existed. But if you don't want Rangel in charge of your healthcare, you're a dumb hater.

Of what—short term memory loss?

The real joke is that liberals like Frank, Waters, Rangel, Pelosi, and Reid really do believe they have the intellectual "street cred" with the American people to win the argument just by showing up. They have no idea how dumb we think—or rather "know"—they are. They're so suffused with the spirit of Joe Biden, the "I probably have a much higher IQ" ethos, they don't even realize most Americans think *they're* the idiots.

Which helps explain why a bunch of "ignorant yokels" on talk radio and at townhall meetings have made such an impact on public policy. When our Dear Leader was sworn in as president on January 20, 2009, it was supposed to herald an era of government by acclamation.

He had an overwhelmingly Democratic Congress and a sycophantic media doing his bidding. So who was going to oppose him? The Republican Party? What party? They were in hiding, and conservatives in general were dismissed as angry, fringe-dwelling cranks.

As for my mom and the rest of the American people, well, you were expected to just sit back and let Obama work his magic. "A nation healed. A world repaired. An America that believes again," as candidate Obama put it.

By 2010, President Obama's agenda was on the ropes. Instead of a steamroller, ObamaCare wheeled through Nancy Pelosi's House of Representatives on a gurney, plugged into life support. Instead of providing Democratic candidates with an electoral Midas Touch, Obama's direct intervention did nothing to help his party's high-profile candidates in New Jersey, Virginia, and Massachusetts—and may have actually hurt them.

Who turned the tide? "Stupid" people, that's who. All you unenlightened citizens who dared to show up at public events with crazy questions about healthcare rationing and your silly signs about how "Nobody Ever Borrowed Their Way Out Of Debt!" Millions of average Americans managed to outsmart the Smartest President Ever®...just by showing up.

Chapter Six

You're Wrong Because You're Right

This exchange is from a revealing conversation I had with liberal author Laura Flanders in late 2009 on the MSNBC network's *The Ed Show*:

> **Flanders:** It's not a problem of just what's happening in these Tea Parties. The lack of respect for people's needs and wishes in this country, it's happening in our Congress. It's not a government takeover of health care. We have our government taken over by people who believe in no government. And they're going to prove that government change can happen, because that's what they were elected to do. They're a wrecking crew. We can't let them wreck our chance for change.

Graham: How can you say they're ignoring the people when only 31 percent of the people in the latest poll support this plan, and more than 50 percent say they don't? It's absolute insanity. You're on another planet.

Flanders: . . . We are seeing a handful of naysayers basically derail our whole process. Americans voted for change.

Graham: Do you not have access to the polls? Are you literate? Do you own a newspaper? Have you not seen the polls on President Obama's performance on health care, on the overwhelming rejection of this? Independents don't like it. Republicans—

MSNBC Host Ed Schultz: Michael, I don't know where you're getting your information.

Graham: I read *Newsweek*!

And sometimes, I even watch MSNBC.

It was on another edition of *The Ed Show*, hosted by the painfully earnest "Big Ed" Schultz, that I got a solid dose of unvarnished leftism. My role once again was to oppose ObamaCare—part of my duties as the show's "token right-wing nut." (That's the unofficial MSNBC euphemism for people whose favorite political philosopher *isn't* Chairman Mao.)

I was waiting in the studio, rehearsing my argument: all the talk of "public options" and "opt outs" and the like was a phony fig leaf to provide cover for wavering moderates so they could give President Obama what he and the far Left really want: a government-run program that would be the first step toward a European-style, single-payer system.

But before I even got in front of the camera, the lefties made my point for me. As I watched the TV monitor in astonishment, the host looked right into the camera and gave away the game. "Harry Reid has given Senate Democrats all the cover they need!" he screamed. (Ed always screams. It's part of his charm.)

"This is a great move by the Democrats," he continued. "This is calling out Senate moderates who aren't too sure about the public option. It's a great move by Harry Reid to put it this way. And it is the first step to single payer. That's what we progressives want. This is just taking the road to get there."

He was joined by liberal Ohio senator Sherrod Brown, who confirmed Ed's confession and added, "Even with an opt out, most states aren't going to opt out. Once you give something to someone, they're not going to give it back."

They sounded like dealers telling their street hoods how to sell crack: *"Just get the voters hooked. Once they're on it, they'll pay and pay and never get off!"*

And there it was, on national TV (well, MSNBC anyway). Team Obama's entire con, laid out for all to see. And it wasn't revealed by FOX News or a *Wall Street Journal* exposé. It was a liberal host and a liberal guest on a liberal network, bragging about the scam to anyone who would listen. Which, this being MSNBC, was mostly a small group of their fellow liberals.

But still—I'm sitting in a studio, waiting to go on national TV, and I'm thinking to myself, "Why do they need me? They just admitted what they've been mocking the tea partiers for saying since Obama got elected."

How many times did we see Democratic politicians and liberal pundits dismiss the "Feds Out of My Meds" signs at tea parties and townhalls as ignorant nonsense? President Obama adamantly denied that ObamaCare aimed at government control of healthcare. "To my Republican friends, I say that rather than making wild claims about a government takeover of healthcare, we should work together to address any legitimate concerns you may have," the president declared before Congress.

It turns out the GOP's biggest "legitimate concern" was, in fact, the government takeover of healthcare.

And you don't just have to take my—and MSNBC's word—for it. Obama's own economic advisor, former labor secretary Robert Reich, admitted that the Democrats' version of ObamaCare "won't offer most Americans any appreciable decline in the cost of their health insurance nor clear improvement in the efficiency or quality of the health care they receive." He added that additional, unnecessary costs from Obama's political deals "will be borne by those Americans who will be required to buy insurance but won't qualify for federal assistance, along with Medicare beneficiaries who will be paying more and receiving less."

I wonder if Reich has a "Keep Your Hands Off My Healthcare" sign, too?

Is it still a con if everyone conning you admits it up front? Or is it just a good, old-fashioned screw job? Either way, by the time Congress got around to voting on ObamaCare, the big-government scam was an open secret.

In fact, some blunt liberals publicly argued that Democrats should lie about the ObamaCare plan if that's what it took to get it passed. Here was John Cassidy, economics writer at the *New Yorker*:

> The U.S. government is making a costly and open-ended commitment to help provide health coverage for the vast majority of its citizens. I support this commitment, and I think the federal government's spending priorities should be altered to make it happen. But let's not pretend that it isn't

a big deal, or that it will be self-financing, or that it will work out exactly as planned. It won't.

Many Democratic insiders know all this, or most of it. *What is really unfolding, I suspect, is the scenario that many conservatives feared.* The Obama Administration, like the Bush Administration before it (and many other Administrations before that) is creating a new entitlement program, which, once established, will be virtually impossible to rescind. At some point in the future, the fiscal consequences of the reform will have to be dealt with in a more meaningful way, but by then the principle of (near) universal coverage will be well established. Even a twenty-first-century Ronald Reagan will have great difficulty overturning it.

That takes me back to where I began. Both in terms of the political calculus of the Democratic Party, and in terms of making the United States a more equitable society, *expanding health-care coverage now and worrying later about its long-term consequences is an eminently defensible strategy.* Putting on my amateur historian's cap, *I might even claim that some subterfuge is historically necessary* to get great reforms enacted. But as an economics reporter and commentator, I feel obliged to put on my green eyeshade and count the dollars. [emphasis added]

"The scenario many conservatives feared"—is that how you put it? Isn't "the scenario millions of Americans protested" more correct? Or maybe "the scenario every commonsense American could see coming a mile away?"

It all comes down to the same thing. The liberals who mocked the tea partiers as conspiracy kooks for claiming ObamaCare was socialized medicine were essentially admitting the kooks were right all along. Those supposedly ignorant yokels and brain-washed hatemongers at the tea parties and townhalls were right, and the dupes in the media who trust the liberal spin were wrong.

Normal Americans were right because the Obama agenda was so obviously and demonstrably wrong. Liberals love to dismiss conservatives as simple-minded and lacking in nuance. Maybe. But what we lack in nuance we make up for in nonsense-aversion. We've had hucksters trying to sell us on get-rich-quick schemes and "No Money Down!" deals our whole lives. So when President Obama promised to turn around the economy by borrowing a trillion dollars and handing it out in government salaries and welfare benefits, we knew it was bogus from the start.

I guess tea party types like my mom aren't quite smart enough to fall for something this stupid. We have a problem dealing with contradiction—that's one reason most of us found philosophy class annoying. Aristotle's "A = A," we're fine with that. Foucault's "A = Nietzsche's dog ate my enigma to punish me for loving him"—not so much.

While the world is full of mystery and wonder, typical Americans have had great success with linear thinking. Lay out your arguments, show us how they make sense. If they don't, then don't do it.

Yeah, yeah, we know some big thinkers have other ideas; Emerson's insistence that "a foolish consistency is the hobgoblin of little minds" and F. Scott Fitzgerald's quip that "a test of a first-rate intelligence is the ability to hold two opposed ideas in the mind at the same time," blah, blah, blah. But to quote another great philosopher, my uncle Arthur Joe of Horry County, South Carolina, "Don't pee down my leg and tell me that it's raining."

When the government tells us simple-minded citizens it will spend money we don't have to "save" jobs it didn't create, and it will give "free" health-care to millions—and it's all going to get paid for by a few wealthy Americans without damaging the economy, we're dubious. We're not saying Team Obama can't do it. We just want a clear, linear answer to the question, "How?"

Love Letter from the Left

"[They are] evil-mongers" spreading "lies, innuendo, and rumor."

—Democratic Senate majority leader Harry Reid, on ObamaCare opponents at townhall meetings.

If the answer we get makes no sense, when it flies in the face of common sense and what we know about the human condition, we get annoyed. And when the answers aren't forthcoming at all, typical Americans know what that means: it's yet another politician who doesn't *have* an answer.

Which is why most typical Americans don't share Fitzgerald's admiration for intellectuals who hold two opposed ideas simultaneously. No, we're more likely to agree with George Orwell's term for that particular talent: "doublethink."

A Self-Stimulating Government

Throughout the debate over Obama's $800 billion "screw-u-lus" package, typical folks like myself simply failed to see the logic of Obama's plans. The financial markets are in crisis. Banks are bleeding money and going out of business. There's a credit crunch—foreclosures are going up. And Team Obama's solution is to give billions to . . . public school teachers?

Nothing against teachers, who are fine people and have a job most of us would only accept as part of a plea bargain. But in the midst of an economic meltdown, the phrase, "Quick—ship more money to the middle school science department!" isn't the first one that springs to mind.

But that's exactly what happened. "Educators Benefit Most from Stimulus Funds" was the headline from the November 2009 AP analysis of where the money went. Other big winners: cops, state government workers, and people on state-funded healthcare.

Now, I'm not disparaging any sick police officers who work part-time at the DMV. I'm simply asking someone to explain to me how that coughing cop was ever going to turn around the economy.

And today, a year after the stimulus passed, the O-bots act surprised that it didn't work. *Of course* it didn't work. *Of course* pouring billions into the pockets of state bureaucrats failed to lower the unemployment rate. *Of course* taking money from productive Americans and giving it to the government didn't create any jobs. I could have told you that before this disastrous, debt-exploding plan was approved. So could the tea partiers. In fact, we did. According to Rasmussen, support for the stimulus bill was just 37 percent before the bill was even enacted. About 50 percent of Americans believed that, over the long run, it would do more harm than good.

But the people and their common-sense questions were ignored. And what happened—besides the 10 percent unemployment, that is? Exactly what townhallers and talk radio listeners predicted: the screw-u-lus package grew more government, generated some low-rent fraud, and put another trillion dollars in debt on the backs of American taxpayers and their children. But as for improving the economy, it was a total flop.

Not that the stimulus didn't provide some entertainment. We all had a good laugh reading news stories about the Southwest Georgia Community Action Council, for example, that used its $1.3 million in stimulus funding to "create or save 935 jobs," according to *USA Today*—a neat trick given that they only have 500 employees. And that they didn't hire anyone with the money. And spent it on raises for people who already had jobs. And reported these bogus numbers using instructions from the Obama administration.

"If I give you a raise, it is going to save a portion of your job," HHS spokesman Luis Rosero said. That's Obamanomics for you: saving or creating hundreds of thousands of "portions" of a job. Can I get the portion that involves going back to work?

Then there's the shoe store owner in Kentucky who "saved or created" nine jobs for just $900. A hundred bucks a job? If we got that kind of performance from the rest of the stimulus money, Obama would have put 7.8 billion Americans to work. Take that, China!

Only, the Kentucky cobbler didn't actually make nine jobs. Instead, he made eighteen boots—nine pairs for members of the Army Corps of Engineers. Jobs reported as "saved or created?" Nine. Actual jobs saved or created? Zero.

According to a Reuters analysis using the White House's own numbers, each job the administration claims to have created cost the taxpayers $246,436. Obviously we'd be better off giving that quarter-million-dollar "worker" $100,000 and sending him home. But since the White House is using fake numbers, anyway—who the hell knows what we're getting for our money?

Or *where* it's going—a problem we discovered when journalists started reviewing White House figures and found millions of dollars going to job creation in New Hampshire's 6th Congressional district (NH-6), along with the AZ-15, CT-42 and U.S. Virgin Island's 99th. This is a true economic miracle, given that none of these districts actually exist. The Virgin Islands, in fact, doesn't have *any* congressional districts.

How did this happen? Who really got the money? To quote Ed Pound, spokesman for President Obama's Recovery.gov website that collected, reviewed, and posted this bizarre information, "Who knows, man, who really knows?"

But typical Americans who opposed the screw-u-lus package *did* know. We knew it would be handed out based on politics, not economics, because politicians were doing the handing. We knew there would be waste, graft, and corruption because we know how government always works. It was a scam from the beginning.

Which brings us to the shamelessly idiotic notion of jobs "created or saved." Can you imagine what the press would have done to Karl Rove if he'd gone on TV and said the Bush tax cuts had "created or saved" even *one* job? They would have eaten him alive. As every economist in the private sector told any reporter who asked, the concept is a joke.

- "One can search economic textbooks forever without finding a concept called 'jobs saved.'"
    —Allan Meltzer, professor of political economy, Tepper School of Business, Carnegie Mellon University
- "A metric has to be measurable, and the actual number of jobs 'created or saved' by the policy will never be measurable from any data source."
    —Greg Mankiw, economics professor, Harvard University.

- "Measuring total jobs 'saved' by a piece of legislation is as difficult as measuring total crimes prevented by police patrols. That's why no agency—not the Labor Department, not the Treasury, not the Bureau of Labor Statistics—actually calculates 'jobs saved.'"
  —Veronique de Rugy, senior research fellow, Mercutus Center, George Mason University.
- "Are you &*$%-ing kidding me?"
  —the guy who pumps my gas.

Taking credit for jobs "saved" is an embarrassingly stupid, economically indefensible, politically ridiculous idea—and it didn't come from a homemade sign at a tea party rally. It came from the White House—the same White House that thinks you're "confused" and your protests against their policies are outrageous.

Average Americans who rejected this avalanche of spending were right. President Obama's top economic advisor, Christina Romer, acknowledged in October 2009 that the stimulus's impact would largely be over by the end of the year. When she said that, unemployment was at 9.8 percent—nearly two whole percentage points higher than she predicted the rate would go if the stimulus were passed.

Congress passed it. Politicians spent it. And we lost about 3 million jobs after it was passed. Unemployment blew past 10 percent. The stimulus was a bust.

Getting It Right

And believe it or not, the $3 billion Cash for Clunkers plan was even worse. The plan was to pay car buyers up to $4,500 to replace perfectly functional cars with new vehicles that got slightly better gas mileage. When it was launched, the car industry publication Edmunds.com predicted that each car that was purchased because of the program—not just a car that would have been bought anyway—would end up costing taxpayers $20,000.

Edmunds was wrong. The final tally was *$24,000* per car.

The plan, being a government program, nearly collapsed in the first week. Congress completely "misunderestimated" car buyers' desire for free money from the taxpayers. So politicians rushed to vote more billions into the program. Computers at car dealers crashed, local businesses waited for the money to arrive, some cars were sold by dealers who couldn't say for sure the federal payoff was even coming through—in other words, just another day in a government-run paradise.

And as for helping the ailing American car industry, C4C had little impact. According to *Automotive News*, U.S. auto sales during the clunkers month of August 2009 were up, "but the increase was modest—a mere 1.0 percent above August 2008."

And where did all the money go? It wasn't to Chrysler and GM, whose sales plummeted around 45 percent in September. No, the big winners were Japan's Subaru and South Korea's Hyundai-Kia, which set sales records thanks to your cash and American-made clunkers. Hundreds of millions of U.S. tax dollars made their way to Tokyo and Seoul, courtesy of President Obama and the Democratic Congress.

And who opposed this brilliant bit of Washington economic policy? Who waved "Crash This Clunker!" signs at tea party rallies? Who told pollsters they opposed the program, wanted it scrapped, and thought it was a mistake?

Once again—you. You may not be the greatest, bestest, superest community organizer ever in the whole wide world, but you know a dumb idea when you hear one.

The White House, in contrast, went so far as to attack Edmunds.com for reporting the final Cash for Clunkers numbers, accusing the publication of "faulty analysis" and claiming that the White House knows more about auto sales than the folks at Edmunds. That's like a politician picking a fight over military strategy with *Jane's Defence Weekly*, or lecturing the girls at BunnyRanch.net on how to get their groove on.

Ah, but it's the *Obama* White House. They're smarter than everybody. They're righter than everybody. Especially when they're not.

Meanwhile, the liberal media continue to dismiss average Americans who are critical of Obamanomics as "angry mobs," "Birthers," and "teabaggers." Nobody in the press is giving "We, the People" credit for predicting what the White House economists and the Smartest President Ever® completely missed.

Remember all the signs about taxes at the rallies? Or all the townhall attendees who complained about tax hikes, only to be told they were stupid—"Don't you know that there are no tax increases for anyone earning less than $250,000?"

Now the real math is finally coming in for Obama's policies of government gigantism—the massive, true costs of healthcare fees, fines, and higher insurance premiums, not to mention tobacco taxes and crushing regulatory costs. Obama's cap-and-trade scheme is a giant hidden tax that would raise costs on everyone. The ObamaCare bills levied taxes on salaries starting at $200,000, and on anyone who had a high-end insurance policy, including low-income workers with premium health benefits (though union members, a primary Democratic constituency, were conveniently given a five-year exemption). ObamaCare would also raise taxes on medical devices regardless of the recipient's income.

And that was before President Obama's 2011 fiscal year budget was released, with a gasp-inducing price tag of $3.8 trillion—the biggest in history. It also added $1.6 trillion in debt—another record—and raised taxes and fees on nearly every taxpayer. According to Brian Riedl of the Heritage Foundation, the Obama budget would raise taxes $2 trillion over the next ten years.

Who was right again? My mom.

Tea partiers were even right about our much-maligned concerns about socialism. We're portrayed as paranoid, McCarthyite throwbacks for that. But actually, after Obama's election, the word "socialist" was in vogue among exuberant mainstream journalists. *Newsweek* ran a cover story soon after Obama's inauguration declaring, "We Are ALL Socialists Now." And I've never heard "paranoid" or "McCarthyite" used to describe *New York Times* reporter Peter Baker, who asked President Obama in March 2009, "The first six weeks have given people a glimpse of your spending priorities. Are you a socialist as some people have suggested?"

Baker didn't mean it in a bad way. Instead, as he explained to the *Washington Post*, "The point is not the label, per se, but the question of whether the times and the solutions under consideration represent some sort of paradigm shift in our national thinking about the role of government in society. In a moment of taxpayer bank bailouts and shifting tax burden proposals and exploding deficits and expansive health care and energy plans, what is the future of American-style capitalism?"

For the record, President Obama denied being a socialist. Then again, he also promised to close Guantanamo Bay within a year, not to raise taxes on anyone earning less than $250,000 per year, and to broadcast the healthcare negotiations on CSPAN.

But then something happened. It turned out that most typical Americans didn't want socialism. Branding President Obama's takeovers of major banks, car makers, and (he hoped) the health-care industry as "socialist" became a political negative, so journalists stopped doing it. (Hmmm...calling a government takeover of private sector industries "socialist." Where did *that* crazy talk come from?)

So the Left tried a new tactic. Instead of acknowledging their support of European-style socialism, they labeled anyone who even used the word "socialist" a conspiracy-addled crank. Or worse. In August 2009, MSNBC commentator Carlos Watson offered this critique:

> Today I want to talk about a word that we're hearing more and more, and that's the word socialist. You hear it from a lot of conservatives these days, that's usually critiquing the President, or more broadly Democrats. And while that's certainly a legitimate critique, there certainly is an ideology that can and should be critiqued at certain times, it also some times is just a kind of a generic conservative bludgeoning tool.
>
> ...But what concerns me is when in some of those town-hall meetings including the one that we saw in Missouri recently where there were jokes made about lynching, etc., you start to wonder whether in fact the word socialist is becoming a code word, whether or not socialist is becoming the new N-word for frankly for some angry upset birthers and others. I hope that's not the case, but it sure does say to you what David Brooks said the other day on TV which is that more credible conservatives have to stand up and say that there's a line that has to be drawn, that there's a line of responsibility that's important, and that extends to the words that we choose...even legitimate words like socialist.

In January, it's "Socialists for Obama." Nine months later when the poll numbers for ObamaCare were tanking, socialism is "the new N-word."

Is President Obama a socialist? Surely he's more of a socialist than the citizens who protest his policies are "terrorists" or "white supremacists." And yet tea party activists have been hit with both those labels by the Left. And nobody is denouncing the liberals who make those charges as "haters." Instead, they're known as "congressmen" and "*New York Times* columnists" and "respected cable news anchors."

So even when citizen protesters and complainers do get a little cranky and start calling names, they're still more accurate than the White House and the mainstream media.

Townhall attendees and tea partiers are not all Republicans, by any means. And they're not necessarily all conservatives. It's a center-right movement, representing America—a center-right nation. But center-right or far-right, on the issues they've almost always been right. As opposed to the Obama elites, who seem to have gotten nearly everything wrong.

Chapter Seven

You Don't Have to Be an Insane, Anti-American, 9/11 Conspiracy Theorist to Support President Obama. (But It Helps.)

S he believes George W. Bush stole the 2000 election from Al Gore and that he used rigged voting machines to steal it from John Kerry in 2004. She signed the 9/11 Truth Petition calling for an investigation into the U.S. government's role in the World Trade Center attack, and she longs for the glory days when the

Soviet Union was still a superpower. And she's got unusual views on Old Glory:

> Our country is founded on a sham: our forefathers were slave-owning rich white guys who wanted it their way. So when I see the American flag, I go, "Oh my God, you're *insulting* me." That you can have a gay parade on Christopher Street in New York, with naked men and women on a float cheering, "We're here, we're queer!"—that's what makes my heart swell. Not the *flag*, but a gay naked man or woman *burning* the flag. I get choked up with pride.

"She" is actress and liberal activist Janeane Garofalo. Oh, and by the way, she thinks *you're* crazy.

In addition to her famous remark about "teabagging rednecks," Garofolo has also referred to tea partiers like my mom as "functionally retarded adults" who suffer from a "neurological problem."

I'm not a psychiatrist and, unlike Ms. Garofalo, I'm not likely to play one on TV, but I have a mental health concept I'd like to run past her: "Projection: the unconscious act of denial of a person's own attributes, thoughts, and emotions, and instead ascribing them to other people."

Ever since our therapist-in-chief offered his diagnosis of the mental state of red staters ("bitter and clingy," said President Obama, though personally I find us more "spicy and full-bodied"), liberals have been questioning the sanity of those of us who refuse to drink the Kool-Aid.

The examples are practically endless. Paul Krugman in the *New York Times* said of the tea party movement, "It doesn't feel right to make fun of crazy people." Former labor secretary Robert Reich wrote an article on the Tax Day tea parties entitled,

"A Short Citizen's Guide to Kooks, Demagogues, and Right-Wingers." The Democratic Congressional Campaign Committee sent out a fundraising letter attacking "tea party nut jobs." Senator John Kerry dismissed the tea party "circus sideshow" as part of the political "fringe."

Even a moderate Republican like Massachusetts senator Scott Brown gets denounced as a "far-right teabagger" by Senator Charles Schumer, merely for committing the sin of not being a Democrat.

It's always the same litany of insults: "extremists," "whack-jobs," "Birthers," "kooks." People who oppose Team Obama's agenda are never merely "uninformed" or "mistaken," no, no, no. You're "crazy." CNN even did an extended report called, "The Psychology of Talk Radio," featuring a Dr. Gail Saltz diagnosing the mental state of talk radio listeners. Too bad she couldn't find some couch time for Jack Cafferty or Rick Sanchez.

As a former political consultant, I certainly understand the strategy. It's a lot easier for the O-bots to scream, "Shut up you Birther freak!" at a townhall than it is to explain to responsible taxpayers how raising the national debt by nearly $2 trillion in a single budget year is a good thing.

But if there was ever a group of people who lacked the credibility to challenge the mental health of others, it is the collection of conspiracy theorists, psychobabbling loonies, and certifiable crazies who populate Obama Nation.

I See Insane People

I happen to have a passing acquaintance with Janeane Garofalo. I appeared with her on Bill Maher's HBO show, and we spent a couple hours afterwards at a Malibu restaurant debating politics and talking comedy. Having run into her a few times since then, I've come to two conclusions.

First, there is a pleasant and intelligent person buried somewhere inside that rude, angry, tattoo-covered exterior. Second, the rational Janeane can't escape this hideous trap because her far-left politics have literally driven her mad. Indeed, it could be argued that being a nut is a requirement for being a member in good standing of the Obama Left.

Don't take my word for it. Ask a liberal.

Pew Research did. A 2009 study by the Pew Forum on Religion and Public Life asked Americans about their beliefs in supernatural phenomena like psychic powers, astrology, and reincarnation. One would expect that liberals, supposedly comprising the intellectual elite, would be less likely to believe in such hocus pocus. But it turns out that in nearly every category, liberals are more willing to embrace New Age nuttiness than conservatives or independents. Liberal Democrats are about twice as likely as conservatives to believe in fortune tellers and astrology, for example, and they are far more willing to believe that ghosts walk among us and that some objects contain "spiritual energy." Liberals are also about 50 percent more likely than conservatives to claim to have spoken to the dead.

Or, as it's known at ACORN, "conducting voter outreach."

Are you really surprised? I know the liberal meme is that conservatives are at church every Sunday waving snakes over Sarah Palin's pastor while he casts demon spirits out of Kenyan witches. But if you're looking for *real* nuttiness, you'll find a far more target-rich environment by looking left.

Sure there are kooks on the Right, in the middle, and just about everywhere else. But they stand out as exceptions. On Team Obama, a person who's presented as some isolated freak nearly always turns out to be the rule.

Speaking of Van Jones...

Why, you remember Van Jones, Obama's former "Green Jobs Czar?" Jones put his whacked out theories to use attacking the enemies of the progressive Left. He accused white environmentalists of "poisoning" minority communities with pollution, and he famously declared that "it's only white kids" who commit atrocities like Columbine.

I once heard him argue that the 9/11 attack stemmed from a Bush administration plot to have the Israeli secret service blow up the World Trade Center in order to destroy incriminating credit card records proving that Dick Cheney was a regular at a transvestite bar in Georgetown.

Okay, okay, I'm kidding. It was actually a *leather* bar.

But seriously folks, as I mentioned before, this kook really did sign the same 9/11 Truther petition Janeane Garofalo did. He was also a longtime acquaintance of Barack Obama, and his serial insanity wasn't enough to disqualify him from a high-profile job in Obama's White House. He only lost that job after Glenn Beck began exposing different aspects of his looniness on a near-nightly basis. And Jones didn't help himself with his pathetic "explanation" that he signed the Truther petition without reading it. (Signs it, but doesn't read it? Forget the White House—send this guy to Congress!)

Now, I know what my liberal friends are saying. "Big deal, Michael. Van Jones was just one guy, and not that big a deal anyway. Who cares?"

And I agree. Jones is just one guy, and the fact that he subscribed to the Rosie O'Donnell School of Physics and Metallurgy ("Fire has never melted steel!") says nothing about American liberalism or the Obama administration.

But the reaction of Team Obama and the liberal establishment to Jones's firing spoke volumes—most of it creepy and bizarre.

"Van Jones Exit Isn't Right-Wing Win, It's an Obama Surrender," was the headline from the *Nation*, one of America's oldest and most prestigious liberal magazines. The author, journalist John Nichols, denied that being a 9/11 Truther was a problem at all. Jones "merely wanted a more serious inquiry" into the 9/11 attacks, Nichols wrote, adding that many "mainstream Democrats" wanted the same thing.

The *New Republic*, hardly a fringe publication for the Left, threw down the gauntlet by essentially declaring, "We're ALL Truthers Now!" The magazine's John McWhorter wrote,

> Jones was wrong, actually, in disavowing his support for 9/11 conspiracy theory. He signed the document, which can only mean that he supports the idea that 9/11 was planned, or that the Bushies knew something more than they have said, or at least that the charge is plausible enough to require investigation. But support for that idea is hardly unknown among people of the left.

And that wasn't all. Although it gently suggested that Jones "could have been more prudent in his associations with antigovernment groups," *Newsweek* argued that being a 9/11 conspiracy kook was no biggie. "It's worth noting that the 'truther' movement accusing the Bush administration of a hand in 9/11 has evolved significantly since 2004," the magazine claimed. "Back then, it was a sizable group of skeptical citizens asking unanswered questions. Only since then has the association turned fringe and angry."

You see? Jones was only a Truther back when Truthering was cool!

At the leftwing website the *Huffington Post*, David Sirota compared critics who demanded Jones's resignation to "lynch mobs in the Old South" and to a "witchhunting band" in colonial Salem. One small difference, David. Witches—unlike lunatic, conspiracy-addled liberals—don't really exist.

And then there was Obama's reaction—which was not to react at all.

If I had been the President of the United States, if I had seen the reports on al Qaeda and 9/11 that President Obama must have seen, if I had heard top-level briefings on the violence and horror of that day and—most profound—if I were sending more troops into harm's way in Afghanistan to keep another 9/11 from happening—I wouldn't have just asked Van Jones to quietly resign over Labor Day weekend; I would have had Jones thrown onto the pavement of Pennsylvania Avenue, his "Green Jobs Now!" pamphlets fluttering behind him. My reaction would be outrage at such idiocy in my White House, and embarrassment that I had invited it in.

But not President Obama. While he didn't defend Jones's trutherism, he never criticized it, either. The day Jones resigned, Obama sent out White House spokesman Robert Gibbs to "thank him for his service." That was it. No other comment.

Why not? Why not denounce this hateful, anti-American lunacy? Is this just Obama's leadership style? Or could it be because the lunatics are running the liberal asylum?

Perhaps prominent liberal blogger Jane Hamsher unintentionally got to the heart of the matter. Van Jones, she wrote, was "thrown under the bus by the White House for signing his name to a petition expressing something that 35 percent of all Democrats believed as of 2007—that George Bush knew in advance about the attacks of 9/11."

Whoa, a third of Democrats are Truthers? According to a Rasmussen poll she linked to—absolutely. In fact, it's worse. Another

30 percent of Democrats in the same poll said they *weren't sure* whether the U.S. government had advance knowledge of the attacks. Maybe we did, maybe we didn't—who are the Democrats to say? That leaves us with a mere 35 percent of Democrats who actually know what happened on 9/11.

Go to a tea party, and the guy with the tin foil hat and the "Flouridated Water Is a UN/Bilderburg Plot!" sign will be shunted to the sidelines. But go to a liberal rally, and the guy who thinks Osama bin Laden works in Dick Cheney's Department of Voting Machine Manipulation and Weather Control is up on the podium. In fact, there's a good chance he works in the White House.

And these are the people calling *us* insane?

Smackdown: Birthers vs. Truthers

No, not all political nuts fall from the ACORN oak. I know MSNBC liberals are obsessed with the so-called "Birthers"—people who insist President Obama was actually born in Kenya or Indonesia or during the Apollo 7 moon landing. Which is why, the Birthers claim, Obama refuses to release his original birth certificate and instead will only release his Certificate of Live Birth. (Or is it the other way around?)

And while the birther conspiracy has given rise to some solid comedy ("What do God and Barack Obama have in common? Neither one has a birth certificate"), the whole issue is silly. The state of Hawaii says Obama was born in Honolulu, and they're the official record keepers and the final legal authority. I'm not going to waste time going over all the evidence, like the contemporaneous newspaper articles mentioning his birth, because rational people don't need to hear it and the Birthers will never believe it.

But there is a huge difference between Birthers and Truthers. Birthers didn't watch President Obama being born on national TV at Kapi'olani Medical Center for Women and Children in Hawaii. The Truthers, on the other hand, have seen the video-tape. Many of them no doubt watched the images live like I did. They've seen the fire, the debris, the scattered body parts and smoking ruins of the World Trade Center. And still they wonder, "Hmmm...What *really* happened on 9/11?"

Birthers refuse to believe what they can't see, while Truthers have seen—and still refuse to believe. And while some Birthers appear to be motivated by an ugly obsession with race, they allege nothing more than political opportunism: that Obama is techni-cally ineligible to serve as president, and he's hiding the evidence for his own benefit.

Compare that to the Truthers, who are making one of the most horrifying allegations in U.S. history, namely that hundreds, if not thousands, of government employees—including many in the mil-itary and/or intelligence community sworn to protect us with their lives—were part of a conspiracy to murder thousands of Ameri-cans for short-term political gain.

Imagine for a moment how low your opinion of America and our democracy must be to believe something so heinous. Now realize that people with these vile, ignorant views make up—according to liberals themselves—a significant portion of the American Left.

I know you O-bots don't like George W. Bush, but do you really believe he's a cold-hearted, calculating murderer of thousands of his fellow Americans? Even more unbelievable, do you believe he has enough loyal followers in the government to keep this secret?

And let's be honest—a vast secret conspiracy to coordinate hijackings and controlled demolitions as a pretext for war?

Please. This is the federal government we're talking about. They can't even pull off a vast, open program of coordinating mail trucks in order to get my Victoria's Secret catalogues to my house on time.

Lunacy: Not a Bug, But a Feature

If we could reduce all the signs and slogans and speeches of every townhall and tea party to their single essential idea, it would be this: "How does this make sense?"

The $787 billion stimulus plan, the trillion-dollar healthcare takeover, the record-setting singe-year surge in our national debt, the bailouts, the mortgage-money give-aways, the massive expansion of government on the backs of the private sector—how will this help make America stronger? How will it help our economy? How will it make America a nation we will be proud for our children to inherit?

How?

From the hundreds of tea partiers I've talked to—and from listening to my mom—I don't believe the tea party movement is ideological. It's not, "Obama can't be right—

Love Letter from the Left

"There is strong evidence that the [9/11] attacks were staged. If they can make *Avatar*, they can make anything."

—former Malaysian prime minister Mahathir Mohamad.

(Okay, Mahatir technically is not on the Left, but his quote so brilliantly captures the coo-coo-land essence of leftwing conspiracy theories that I made him an honorary leftist just for this chapter.)

he's a Democrat!" Plenty of Democrats, and even more independents, are part of this effort. It's not a coincidence that President Obama's poll numbers among moderates fell as the tea party movement surged.

The Obama elites and their media sycophants often complain about the "angry mob" that opposes them. But they rarely try to understand where the dissatisfaction comes from. They've already got an answer: racism. But that's wrong. The reason so many Americans are concerned—concerned enough to get politically active for the first time—is because they're afraid. And where does that fear come from? From uncertainty, from questions, from not knowing.

And so, typical Americans flooded townhalls and called talk radio shows looking for answers to the question that left them feeling uncertain, fearful for our future: "How?"

Unfortunately, these typical Americans often left even more worried and more fearful, because they couldn't get an answer. They got insults, and plenty of them. They got spin and posturing, they got sincere statements from pliable politicians that all this government spending and re-engineering of the American character is being done with good intentions. And it probably is.

But nobody ever explained *how it's actually supposed to work.*

And now I wonder if Team Obama can even hear that question when it's asked. President Obama explains the math of ObamaCare essentially by saying, "We can have the magic healthcare fairies do tonsilectomies on your children in their sleep and leave the tonsils under the pillow." You say, "That's just crazy—who's going to believe that?" Then you'll turn on your TV and open your newspaper and find out that, not only do people believe it, but you're expected to believe it, too. And if you don't, you're a hatemongering lunatic.

You show up at a townhall meeting because you want to point out what a pile of economic excrement Washington is spreading, and your congressman gets the facts of the plan he voted for completely wrong. Having admitted he never read the plan, he refuses to take questions from the general public, but only "pre-approved" members of the audience who, by sheer coincidence, are all wearing SEIU t-shirts.

After an hour of this fatuous, fact-free spinning, you finally stand up and ask why regular citizens can't speak, why you can't ask the obvious questions about how unworkable the plan is... and immediately people start shouting, "It's a crazed teabagger—somebody taze him, quick!"

Liberal congressmen don't understand why we can't just get with the program and have some faith in their plans. Well, sorry, but we don't believe in genies. Give us some straight answers, or we'll replace you with someone who will.

Cold, Hard Facts

I once had an epiphany watching a videoclip of Al Gore at a global warming event. Irish journalist Phelim McAleer asked Gore to explain erroneous claims about polar bears made in Gore's (so-called) documentary, *An Inconvenient Truth*. Despite Gore's warnings of an imminent polar bear apocalypse, there are actually more polar bears today than when the documentary was released. So McAleer asked Gore a specific question: how do you explain your claims?

Gore answered with a question: "Do you believe polar bears are endangered?"

McAleer answered with a fact: "The number of polar bears have increased."

Gore quickly shot back, "Do you believe polar bears are endangered?"

McAleer again answered, "The number of polar bears have increased."

Now Al Gore became the inquisitor. "Do you believe," he demanded, "that polar bears are endangered?"

A moment's uncomfortable pause, and again: "The number of polar bears have increased," and the audience laughed. Then McAleer's mic was cut off and Gore resumed with the wild, unsubstantiated claims that make him a rock star on the Left.

I watched that exchange several times in a row. It fascinated me, but I couldn't tell why. I repeatedly played the audio on my radio show, simply because I found it so compelling. Then finally, one day it hit me. In this exchange, the great divide between the Obama elites and the average American was laid out before me, and I hadn't seen it.

McAleer was a guy trying to make the math work. He wanted to know how to reconcile Gore's panic-stricken jeremiads about polar bear extinction with facts like the rising polar bear population and the lack of any warming since 1998.

Al Gore, on the other hand, neither offered facts nor asked for them. He showed no interest in factual statements or statistics of any kind. All Gore wanted to know was what the questioner *believed* in.

Do you believe polar bears are in trouble? Do you believe in global warming? Do you believe the world would be a better place if rich, conservative businessmen were dragged out of their limos, beaten with biodegradable canes, and forced to bike to work? (As opposed to rich liberal environmentalist kooks, who are welcome to fly private jets to Copenhagen and limo their way to UN conferences.)

Al Gore isn't going to waste time proving things to you. If you need proof, you're not really a believer, are you?

The whole leftwing worldview is based on a suspension of disbelief. Can anyone point to any place in the world where socialism has worked? Where a collective economy based on liberal theories of "social justice" has actually fed, clothed, and housed people, and done so as well as capitalism? No. It's never happened.

Do people ever leave America for advanced treatment in Cuba or even in Canada? Is there an example anywhere of socialized medicine leading the way in new treatments, pharmaceuticals, or medical technologies? No. But the O-bots demand we believe their healthcare "reform" will do it. We must stop doubting and abandon our selfish cynicism. We gotta have faith!

And has there been an example yet of appeasement and unilateral disarmament convincing dangerous regimes to quit acting like thugs? Not one. And yet we're told that Iran, North Korea, and other miscreants are only reacting to our militaristic behavior. Why can't we just talk to the ayatollahs, trust them, and stop judging them and their whackjob, anti-Semitic policies?

Must you look at the world as it is, liberals ask? Why not see the world as you wish it to be?

Unfortunately, many of us simpleton Americans are stuck with that old standby, reality.

Some Democrats still want us to believe that the way to fix healthcare is to make millions of Americans into new Medicare patients while simultaneously cutting the Medicare budget by $500 million. The program's already going broke, you're going to add millions of patients while cutting billions of dollars—and you think it will *fix* the problem?

That isn't "starry-eyed optimism," that's just jaw-dropping stupidity.

And one must have the faith of a child (and the brains of a cardboard box) to trust the estimated future costs of ObamaCare. Even if the O-bots' math were right today (and it's not), who is naïve enough to believe this trillion-dollar government program will come in on budget? I know people who believe in leprechauns and the Tooth Fairy who aren't that gullible.

As for me, I don't believe we need to abolish the internal combustion engine and stop cows from farting in order to save the Earth.

I don't believe we can get information from mass-murdering terrorists by giving them lawyers and all the rights of U.S. citizens.

I don't believe in invisible jobs "saved" by magic "stimulus" money in Neverland's 99th Congressional District.

Compared to my liberal friends, I'm a hyper-rational, flint-hearted cynic—all I believe in is Santa Claus.

Chapter Eight

Watching the Wrong Cable News

"The genius of Roger Ailes and Rupert Murdoch is that they've discovered a niche audience for American broadcast news, namely, half of the American people."

—Charles Krauthammer, on the success of FOX News

f liberals were vampires, they wouldn't fear sunlight. Instead, we'd kill them with the FOX News Channel.

How much do liberals hate FOX? In 2009, four members of the YMCA in Ipswich, Massachusetts, published a letter in a local newspaper complaining that folks on the ellipticals were watching FOX on the overhead TV. Although you need headsets to hear the TV, sweaty Obama supporters objected to the club simply allowing this evil cable news channel to be turned on. Decrying the "scrolling headlines and angry expressions" they saw on FOX, the offended complainants argued that "the fact that the Ipswich Y is still supporting the airing of angry, nonsensical debate is still at odds with the organization's mission."

FOX News—so powerful that even *being around people who want to watch it* is unbearable.

I would love to dismiss this handful of East Coast, gated-community liberals as a few fringe nutballs who are not indicative of the attitudes and values of the Obama White House. But what, then, to do with actual members of the Obama White House who feel the same way?

For, about the same time FOX-fearing libs in Massachusetts were fleeing their Thighmasters, White House senior advisor David Axelrod, chief of staff Rahm Emanuel, and then communications director Anita Dunn were launching what the *New York Times* called the "War on FOX News." Dunn introduced the main theme of the war: "What I think is fair to say about FOX—and certainly it's the way we view it—is that it really is more a wing of the Republican Party.... Let's not pretend they're a news network the way CNN is."

In a breathtaking display of courage, Dunn boldly made this claim . . . on CNN.

A few days later, Emanuel also appeared on what was known in the '90s as the Clinton News Network: "The way the president looks at it—we look at it—[FOX] is not a news organization so much as it has a perspective." That same day, Axelrod told *ABC News*, "[FOX] is not really a news station. It's not just their commentators but a lot of their news programming, it's really not news, it's pushing a point of view."

Emanuel and Axelrod then both went on to warn CNN, ABC, the *New York Times*, and all other media outlets not to cross the

White House by treating FOX like a legitimate news organization. "The bigger thing is, other news organizations, like yours,
ought not to treat them that way. We're not going to treat them
that way," Axelrod said.

The White House's call for a boycott of FOX News was music
to the ears of lefty organizations like MoveOn.org. "To draw
attention to its biased coverage, President Obama will not appear
on FOX for the rest of this year," MoveOn.org wrote to its members. "Can you sign this petition asking Democrats to support
President Obama's stance by staying off FOX as long as he does?"

President Obama appeared to mean it, too. That September he
granted interviews to all the Sunday news shows—except FOX.
The White House then informed FOX not to expect any presidential interviews for the rest of 2009.

Love Letter from the Left

"Conservatism will not recover as a coherent governing philosophy until it takes this monstrous propaganda [Sean
Hannity and FOX News] on. Conservatism will not somehow emerge through the wreckage of this current
moment, until it finds the courage to note that what it has
become is not some variant on its tradition rightly understood, but its conscious, active, pernicious nemesis. And
yes, this makes the actual, living breathing representative
of political conservatism in our time the current president
of the United States."

—blogger Andrew Sullivan, denouncing FOX News so vehe-
mently that he opens a portal to a parallel universe where
Barack Obama is a conservative

Not long after, the Obama administration offered to allow a key Treasury Department official to be interviewed by the White House press pool on the condition that FOX—a member of that pool—be excluded. No other White House in history had tried to ostracize a news outlet like that. The assault was so shameless that even liberal media outlets like CBS and CNN objected, forcing the White House to back down. President Obama had a sit down with FOX correspondent Major Garrett in November.

But just to ensure everyone got the message, the Obama administration posted an official "FOX Lies" website where paid employees of the president posted attacks and insults about the number-one rated cable news channel. Somewhere, someone's White House ID may have read, "Department of We Really Hate FOX News."

Think about all this for a second. The White House—residence of the most powerful government in the world, home of the "nuclear football," guarantor of freedom around the world—launched an official attack website targeting a private news organization. In *America*.

Rumors that the Obama administration's "FOX Lies" website was designed by Hugo Chavez could not be confirmed before this book went to press.

Fair and Balanced

I'm not going to defend FOX's news standards because they don't need defending. Is FOX News "objective"? By the standards of a professional scientist conducting research in a bubble suit and hermetically-sealed clean room, no. But by the standards of contemporary journalism—i.e., the *New York Times*, CBS, and MSNBC—absolutely. In reality, FOX easily exceeds those standards every day.

Remember *CBS News* using forged documents as the source of its "coverage" of George W. Bush's service in the Texas Air National Guard? Or the *New York Times*'s "coverage" of those forgeries with the infamous "Fake But Accurate" headline? A story so lousy the *Times* was forced to run a correction... and then a correction of the correction?

Or perhaps you were watching the MSNBC "news" report on the "angry white men" who showed up at President Obama's August 2009 appearance in Arizona. If you did, you saw this exchange:

Dylan Ratigan: Alright, guns at townhall rallies, you're probably familiar. Well, people continue to do it, packing heat at these health care protests. Contessa has the latest. What's going on?

Contessa Brewer: Yeah, we are closely following here, Dylan, townhalls and other events around the country today to see who shows up and what they bring with them. More than 20 town halls scheduled from east-to-west, Virginia to Washington state. Yesterday, as President Obama addressed the Veterans of Foreign Wars in Phoenix. A man at a pro-health care reform rally just outside, wore a semi-automatic assault rifle on his shoulder and a pistol on his hip.... And the reason we're talking about this, a lot of talk here, Dylan, because people feel like, yes, there are Second Amendment rights for sure but also there are questions about whether this has racial overtones. I mean, here you have a man of color in the presidency and white people showing up with guns strapped to their waists or to their legs.

Toure [MSNBC pop culture analyst, and guy with one name]: It sounds simplistic when you put it that way, but it is real that there is tremendous anger in this country about government, the way government seems to be taking over the country, anger about a black person being president. Just several upheavals in the country over the last ten years from 9/11, to the economic tsunami, to the black man becoming president and, you know, we see these hate groups rising up and this is definitely part of that.

Brewer: So do you—do you think if Barack Obama were white, though, that you would not see people showing up— let's say if it were Bill Clinton—you would not see people showing up with weapons strapped to their legs?

Toure: You know, I don't know. I don't know. That—I mean, that's hard to say. It is unknowable. But you do see a rise in hate group activity throughout the country. . . . I'm not going to be surprised if we see somebody get a chance and take a chance and really try to hurt him or really—you know, and I mean it's up to the Secret Service to make sure that it doesn't actually become history, but, you know, I think we're going to see somebody, you know, some sort of Squeaky From, some sort of Mark [sic] Hinckley figure, because there's so much anger in the country about him, about what's going on with government.

Ratigan: Angry at government and racism, you put those two together.

Terrifying, isn't it? I know I go to bed every night in fear that another "Mark Hinkley figure" may be among us. Or perhaps a Mitch Harvey Oswalk or—horrors!—Dave Wilkes Booth.

One thing the "reporters" at MSNBC failed to mention, however, is that the guy toting that rifle and wearing a pistol on his hip, the specific guy they were talking about in the "white people showing up with guns strapped to their waists" part of the story...was *black*.

And they were showing videotape of him at the time.

How do you show video of a black guy with a gun and still describe him as a racist white guy—perhaps even the next "Mark" Hinkley? By doing what MSNBC did, and carefully editing the video so the man's face, hands, and skin are never seen. The producers at MSNBC knew he was black, and they deliberately duped their audience.

I don't want to promote violence, but this crap is enough to turn some disgruntled viewer into the next Reginald McVeigh.

Let me be clear here. I'm not saying, "What's the big deal about FOX? They're biased to the Right the way MSNBC is biased to the Left." Sorry—that's just not true. I'm saying that FOX News is less biased and more objective than CNN, MSNBC, CBS, and the others. FOX just looks like it's rightwing because the other news organizations are so far to the Left.

I hate it when conservatives say, "We've got FOX, liberals have got everything else," as if there's some equivalent level of bias between the two sides. Really? Show me the example of FOX News misrepresenting someone's racial identity, or attributing fake quotes to someone for purely political purposes, as routinely happens to Rush Limbaugh. When have you ever seen FOX defend a story as "fake but accurate"?

FOX isn't perfect. Nobody is. People sometimes get stuff wrong, and I'm no exception. But if innocent mistakes were the only problem with "news" outlets like CBS and Reuters, I wouldn't be writing this chapter.

The problem is that the leftwing bias in the mainstream media is so innate, so much a part of their DNA, that they don't even realize it. Most conservatives scoff when the MSM claims they're not biased, but I think they really believe it—they simply think that liberal viewpoints and policies are objectively, indisputably right, so that's what they report. And because they refuse to acknowledge their bias, of course, they make no effort to fight it.

"Bias? What Bias?"

There was a classic moment in 2009 when the *New York Times*, having missed the Van Jones 9/11 Truther story until after he'd resigned, and also having missed the entire ACORN/child prostitution story, finally investigated why the paper's readers were the last ones hearing the news.

"Some editors told me they were not immediately aware of the Acorn videos on FOX, YouTube and a new conservative Web site called BigGovernment.com," *Times* ombudsman Clark Hoyt wrote. "When the Senate voted to cut off all federal funds to Acorn, there was not a word in the newspaper or on its Web site. When the New York City Council froze all its funding for Acorn and the Brooklyn district attorney opened a criminal investigation, there was still nothing."

But don't worry, Hoyt insisted, the problem isn't bias. It just looks that way: "Some [conservative media] stories, lacking facts, never catch fire. But others do, and a newspaper like the Times needs to be alert to them or wind up looking clueless or, worse, partisan itself."

Really, Clark? The problem is "LOOKING" partisan? That's it?

So what was it just a few weeks later when the Climategate scandal broke? Emails were leaked showing premier scientists in the movement for global-warming alarmism had tried to exclude opposing views from peer-researched journals, colluded to hide their raw data, and threatened the destruction of information to avoid legal disclosure requirements.

Another liberal scandal, well-covered on the internet and FOX News—and totally ignored by the *New York Times* for weeks.

So what's the solution? According to Hoyt, in order to keep up with those weird rightwing stories, *Times* editors assigned someone to watch other news outlets and brief editors on what they were covering. What other news outlets? FOX News, for one.

Now, I'll admit the phrase "trusted source for the *New York Times*" isn't the endorsement it once was. I doubt it will appear on FOX's credits. All I can do is report. You decide.

Meanwhile, studies confirm FOX News is, at the very least, as objective as its competitors. For example, a Pew Research study of the 2008 presidential election found that, in the final six weeks of the campaign, FOX ran nearly an identical percentage of negative stories about Obama and McCain (40 percent). But at CNN, there were 22 percent more negative stories about McCain than Obama. At MSNBC, 73 percent of the stories about John McCain were negative. The percentage of negative Obama stories? 14 percent—a *59 point, pro-Obama bias.*

As Robert Lichter, head of the Center for Media and Public Affairs, admitted to the Associated Press on the eve of the 2008 election, "For whatever reason, the media are portraying Barack Obama as a better choice for president than John McCain. If you watch the evening news, you'd think you should vote for Obama."

And the White House is trying to silence FOX News? If they were smart, they'd be *on* FOX News. As Democratic consultant and unapologetic liberal Bob Beckell told FOX, "The Obama administration should be here on Fox, because you can talk to more independents and Democrats here than on any of the other networks."

Then there was this confession by Julia Piscitelli, progressive political strategist, writing at her *US News & World Report* blog: "Hi, my name is Julia, I am a Democrat, and I appear on FOX. Dems, I hate to break it to you, but not only is FOX the No. 1 cable news station, they actually put more women on as experts during the day than MSNBC or CNN."

She's right. FOX also books a more equal number of liberals and conservatives. That's one reason why Pew's study of the 2008 election found FOX to be one of the most balanced sources covering the race. That makes sense, given that another Pew study found that FOX's audience is the least partisan of the three news networks. Only 39 percent of FOX viewers are Republicans, while Democrats make up 45 percent of MSNBC's audience and a whopping 51 percent of CNN's. Over at FOX, 55 percent of the audience is either Democratic or independent.

But the demonization of FOX continues, and I'm not talking about just the overt lunatics like Keith Olbermann or Rick Sanchez. I'm talking about once-legitimate news outlets like *Time* magazine, where Joe Klein wrote, "FOX News peddles a fair amount of hateful crap. Some of it borders on sedition. Much of it is flat out untrue." And this was in a column *condemning* the White House's "War on FOX."

So there you have the liberal spin: FOX News—they may be hateful, lying traitors, but let them stay on the air anyway.

How magnanimous.

Sarah's Story

One glaring example of media bias is its coverage of Sarah Palin. It's safe to say that mainstream media outlets had more reporting errors about Palin in the month after John McCain nominated her than FOX News has had this decade. And I'm not talking about the lunacy spread by prominent liberals like Andrew Sullivan regarding Palin's alleged fake pregnancy. I mean simple, easy-to-check stories that the MSM got wrong and, sadly, rarely bothered to correct. (No, Palin was never a member of the Alaska Independence Party; no, she didn't try to get evolution banned from public schools; no she never called the Iraq War "God's will.")

If FOX had a record of misreporting even close to this, trust me—everyone would know about it. The networks and the White House would make absolutely sure.

Instead, FOX-o-phobia is so rampant that, when one lib dared to defend FOX on NPR (your government-run radio network), he was forced to apologize for it.

Here's the story: soon after the White House launched its "War on FOX," NPR political editor Ken Rudin remarked about it, "It's not only aggressive, it's almost Nixonesque." Rudin also committed the sin of exposing the Left's hypocrisy:

> Of course, then it was a conservative president denouncing a liberal media, and of course, a lot of good liberals said, "Oh, that's ridiculous. That's an infringement on the freedom of press." And now you see a lot of liberals almost kind of applauding what the White House is doing to FOX News, which I think is distressing.

The reaction from government-run radio's liberal audience was swift, as Byron York reported in the *Washington Examiner*: "Within 24 hours, Rudin was in backtrack mode."

Rudin called his own comments "a bonehead mistake," adding, "I apologize for a dumb comparison." This earned him a pat on the head from NPR ombudsman Alicia Shepard, who wrote, "I applaud Rudin for quickly apologizing. Journalists are going to make mistakes. . . . Acknowledging them goes a long way to maintaining credibility."

Oh, yeah, Ken Rudin's "credibility" is through the roof now. I'd trust him way over, say, Brit Hume, Chris Wallace, or Wendell Goler.

What's funny about the Left's obsession with FOX News is that, if you talk to tea partiers or talk radio listeners, you'll find that most of them have an eclectic mix of news sources. Yes, FOX does well, but talk radio listeners are far bigger consumers of news in general than the public at large. They also tend to be more informed about current events than Americans as a whole.

Back in 1996, an Annenberg study found that "political talk radio listeners are more likely than non-listeners to consume all news media other than TV news, to be more knowledgeable, and to be involved in political activities." And I already mentioned the 2006 Pew survey, which found that two of the most informed groups of media consumers in America are Rush Limbaugh listeners and Bill O'Reilly viewers. Talk radio listeners as a whole knew more about what's going on than viewers of PBS's *News Hour*, regular daily newspaper readers, or the seven remaining CNN viewers.

Now, it's true that FOX viewers as a whole scored much lower. And when a Pew study came out showing viewers of Comedy Central's *Daily Show* and the *Colbert Report* outscored FOX viewers on current events, liberal bloggers delighted in posting headlines like, "How Dumb are FOX Viewers?"

What was largely overlooked is the fact that *Daily Show* and *Colbert* viewers outscored *everyone*—including newspapers, news weeklies, and every news network. But when I Googled that story I couldn't find a single headline asking, "How Dumb are MSNBC Viewers?"

Meanwhile, two of the groups that scored just below the *Daily/Colbert* tandem were, once again, O'Reilly and Limbaugh fans.

While the relative intellects of the viewers of various cable news channels may be debatable, here's something that's not: FOX News absolutely whips its competitors. And I mean *whips*, routinely tripling and even quadrupling the viewership of the liberal networks. According to *Broadcasting & Cable,* in the third quarter of 2009 FOX ranked fourth among cable networks—not just among news channels, we're talking *all* cable networks. Meanwhile, CNN and MSNBC ranked 21st and 25th, respectively.

In fact, FOX News often has more viewers in a week than CNN, Headline News, and MSNBC combined. Part of that comes from trust: a 2010 poll showed FOX was the most trusted TV news outlet.

So Anita Dunn was right when she said FOX News isn't like CNN or MSNBC.

People actually watch FOX News.

Chapter Nine

Barack Obama: As Smart as Sarah Palin?

I don't know whether or not liberal elitists believe in God, but I'm absolutely sure they believe in the Devil. And they call her Sarah Palin.

I've been following politics at some level since I was a 10-year-old singing song parodies about the Ford administration into my dad's cassette recorder. (You don't want to know.) I spent six years running political campaigns, including bare-knuckle GOP primaries in Lee Atwater's South Carolina. I even worked on a Republican congressional campaign in Chicago. In short, I've just about seen it all.

But I have *never* seen a political figure thrashed, trashed, and cashed (in on, that is) like Sarah Palin.

If a conservative politician ever treated a liberal woman the way the Obama elites treat Sarah Palin, he'd be denounced by every paper in the country. If a radio talk host gave Hillary Clinton or Nancy Pelosi the Palin Treatment, the National Organization of Women would have stoned him to death by an NCAA women's volleyball team.

And if a local man treated Sarah that way in Alaska? Her rifle barrel would be warm and the body would never be found.

I say this as a conservative who never jumped on the Palin bandwagon. My candidates have been more on the Buckley/ George Will end of the conservative spectrum. In fact, when John McCain picked Palin to be his running mate, I immediately admitted she wasn't ready for the job.

"Governor Palin does not have enough executive experience to be vice president," I said at the time. "She just has more than Barack Obama."

That indisputable statement launched torrents of foaming-mouthed invective from the Left. A liberal friend of mine sincerely questioned my sanity—even after conceding that, technically speaking, I was right on the facts. Didn't matter. Respectable people simply didn't say nice things about "that woman."

A single sentence of backhanded praise for Palin (she had a 90 percent approval rating in Alaska at one point), and the Obama elite suddenly turned into Linda Blair from the *Exorcist*. I joked during one interview that I was going to have to start wearing a rain coat to keep the spittle off my clothes from the ranting, bulging-eyed Palin-haters in the media.

Have you heard what Obama supporters and media hatchetmen call Sarah Palin in public? Listing the vile, vulgar, and outright sexist slurs against this mother of five would fill the New York City phonebook. It also would be a bestseller in Manhattan, snatched

up by self-declared liberal feminists on the Upper West Side glee-
fully skimming the pages looking for words rhyming with "bunt."

It would be easier to list what they *didn't* call Governor Palin.
For example, "governor." It's fascinating to Google columns from
liberal writers covering the 2008 election and compare how often
one-term senator Barack Obama's name was prefaced by "Senator," as opposed to how often one-term—and wildly successful—
Governor Palin was just called "Palin." If she was lucky.

I'm not saying Sarah Palin was or is ready to be president or
vice president. I'm not saying you have to admire her, or even
like her. In fact, I'm not even asking O-bots to stop hating her,
though it might be a smart tactical move. I don't know if the
Obama elites have noticed, but the more they hate her, the higher
her approval ratings rise. I'm just saying that during the 2008
presidential campaign, she had a better resume than the former
community organizer.

Why do you loathe her so, my liberal friends? What did she
ever do to you? She wasn't Rush Limbaugh, slaughtering leftwing
sacred cows before an audience of tens of millions. She was in
Alaska, cutting taxes and attacking the Republican establishment.
Has it occurred to you that Sarah Palin's done more to put corrupt Republicans in jail than Eric Holder?

Palin was no Mitt Romney or Mike Huckabee, either. She
wasn't out on the campaign trail declaring she would be a better
president than your guy. And here's a reminder: Sarah Palin *didn't
run* for president. She didn't put herself out there to run for anything. All she did was answer a phone call from John McCain
and say "yes" to his request.

And Team Obama went totally, bat-snot crazy.

I understand, my dear lib, that you probably don't know very
much about Governor Palin. A post-election Zogby poll, for

example, showed most liberals believed Palin actually said, "I can see Russia from my house!" (It was Tina Fey on *Saturday Night Live*.)

Chances are, you only know what the lunatic media Left told you about her, which means you aren't just uninformed, you're *misinformed*. As Matthew Continetti wrote in his book *The Persecution of Sarah Palin*,

> If you listened to Democrats and the mainstream media, you learned that Palin was a Buchananite (she wasn't), a member of the Alaskan Independence Party (nope), and a biblical literalist who believed dinosaurs roamed the earth several thousand years ago (an utter fabrication); that she was anti-contraception (incorrect), wanted to teach creationism in schools (not really), and didn't believe man may be contributing to global warming (untrue); that she banned books (a gross distortion), claimed she could see Russia from her house (never happened), faked her pregnancy (unbelievable), slept with her husband's business associate (a myth), thought the Iraq war was a mission from God (not so), and didn't know that Africa was a continent (baloney).

And to add to the list, Sarah Palin didn't try to ban the teaching of evolution in Alaskan schools, and no, her pastor never tried to cast a demon spirit out of a witch on videotape.

However, reports that her longtime pastor preached that AIDS was invented by the white supremacist U.S. government to kill black people and that 9/11 was America's "chickens coming home to roost" cannot be confirmed or denied.

If sane people ever retake control of the mainstream media, someone will write a great book about the death of journalistic integrity, and the cover will be Sarah Palin.

And the question remains: why is it that Sarah Palin drives you allegedly tolerant, diversity-loving, mild-mannered liberals into some bizarre form of political 'roid rage? Or in Sarah's case, "estrogen rage." I'm just amazed she got through the campaign without lefty Senator Arlen Specter telling her to "be quiet" and "act like a lady."

Still, I don't get it. After all, she's just a politician.

"But Michael—she's a politician I don't agree with!" So what? If you haven't noticed, my liberal Democrat friends, there's an entire political party whose members disagree with *your* policies (other than senators from Maine, anyway). So Palin's a conservative—so what? I don't remember you getting this screaming mad even when Pat Buchanan ran for office.

"But Michael—she's so stupid!" Okay, let's say for the sake of argument that Sarah's a dummy. What makes her stand out from all the other stupid politicians? "Well, she could have been vice president!" Okay, why don't you re-read my section on Joe Biden, and then argue to me about the crucial importance of having a smart vice president.

"Yeah, but Michael—she's an extremist! A threat to our democracy!" Let me get this straight: liberals who happily elect Nancy Pelosi, Barney Frank, Dennis Kucinich, Al Franken, and self-declared Socialist Bernie Sanders—and who invite Al Sharpton and Michael Moore to your national conventions—are offended by *extremism*?

Love Letter from the Left

"Her greatest hypocrisy is in her pretense that she is a woman."

—*Washington Post* blogger Wendy Doniger, on Sarah Palin

To paraphrase Barry Goldwater, extremism in defense of partisanship may or may not be a virtue. But it's definitely not news.

Sarah Palin isn't a classic cookie-cutter politician, I concede that point. She had an unusual route to power, jumping from PTA to mayor to governor to VP pick. But it's not *that* unusual.

Ronald Reagan went from an actor and SAG leader to governor and one of the greatest American presidents of all time. More recently, Al Franken went from lousy SNL comic to even worse radio talk show host to an abysmal U.S. senator from Minnesota.

Or take the strange case of Hillary Rodham You-Know-Who, a.k.a. "Mrs. Bill Clinton"—depending on the political circumstances of the moment. Mrs. Bill had never held elective office before running for the position of New York senator. She had never lived in New York. She knew so little about the state that she spent part of her time campaigning for votes in Erie, *Pennsylvania*. (That is not a joke. It's a fact. As is so often the case with the Clinton family, however, it's hard to tell the difference.)

But she was elected to the Senate entirely on the fact that she was a woman (*Harold* Clinton would have had no shot at that seat), and because she was married to Bill (you think Hillary Rodham *Johnson* would have had a chance?) With one unimpressive term in the Senate, she then ran for president.

Anyone mad about that?

Not everyone takes the traditional path to power, but nobody's ever inspired the hair-on-fire hatred from the Left that Sarah Palin has. Once again—why?

Brawl on the Mall

Inexperienced, stupid, unqualified, an oddball. I know at least one liberal politician who has been described by his opponents that way repeatedly during his career—and based on legitimate evidence, too. And you know where he lives today?

1600 Pennsylvania Avenue.

What?! Do I dare compare psycho Sarah to the Great and Powerful O? Have I lost all reason? Did I pick up Willie Nelson's brownie order by mistake?

Not at all. In fact, I am prepared to argue that America would be better off today if we had elected President Palin in 2008 instead of President Obama. A Palin presidency would have been demonstrably better for America than what we have now.

Let me once again remind everyone that Governor Palin wasn't running for president. And yet, if you recall the 2008 campaign, you know that O-bots were constantly comparing her with Obama—and for obvious reasons. There was no way anyone could compare the experience, accomplishments, and public service of John McCain and Barack Obama with a straight face.

Obama's allies picked the fight with Palin to try and avoid the cringe-inducing comparisons at the top of the 2008 tickets. So the Obama vs. Palin comparison isn't a fair one to begin with. Unlike the inexperienced, untested, "I vote present" candidate Obama, Palin wasn't asking anyone to make her president. Just the running mate.

But fair or not, I am prepared to take the challenge anyway. Obama vs. Palin...for the White House! LET'S GET READY TO R-R-R-R-R-UMBLE!

Bottom line: if we'd elected Sarah Palin, we'd still have the $787 billion we blew on the stimulus package that flopped even by the bogus "saved or created jobs" standard; went overwhelmingly to white-collar government employees and welfare benefits; and put an additional debt burden of $10,000 on every American family.

That's a knockout blow right there. Oh—you want more? Okay.

If we had elected President Palin in 2008 instead of President Obama, the White House wouldn't have been forced to back down from its idiotic plan to grant 9/11 mastermind Khalid Sheikh Mohammed a trip to New York City and the chance for an international show trial. That's because Sarah Palin never would have proposed such a moronic move in the first place. Instead, KSM would be on his way to 72-Virgin-ville, because President Palin would have allowed the military tribunal authorized by a bipartisan congressional vote to do its job.

Even more important, if we had elected Sarah Palin, the Jockstrap Jihadist who successfully boarded a Christmas Day flight to Detroit would not (as of this writing) be sitting in his attorney's office working on a plea bargain. He wouldn't have been granted Miranda rights as though he were a U.S. citizen, rather than the unlawful enemy combant/Islamist dirtbag whackjob that he is. Only President Obama is "smart" enough to leave an intelligence asset snoozing in a jail cell with the right to remain silent while his al Qaeda pals are plotting their next attack.

Not President Palin. If she had been in office Christmas Day 2009, the Underwear Bomber would have celebrated New Year's Eve having his tender bits lit up like fireworks by a real-life Jack Bauer in Gitmo.

That's it, the referee has stopped the fight. Go home. You can't win…What? You O-bots want another piece of me?

President Palin wouldn't have a tax cheat overseeing the IRS. There would never have been a 9/11 Truther in her administration, either. She never would have set up a White House website for citizens to rat out their friends' "fishy" emails and websites. Nobody would have shouted, "You lie!" because she wouldn't have given a disingenuous hour-long speech accusing the people who disagreed with her of being dishonest and immoral.

Seriously, I can do this all day. Why not just concede now? No? Okay.

President Palin wouldn't have pushed a massive carbon tax ("cap and trade") on businesses in the middle of a job-killing recession. GM and Chrysler would still be the financial disasters they are now, but we taxpayers wouldn't be out the $50 billion Obama blew on them up front, or the billions we're still paying today.

Cash for Clunkers wouldn't have crashed after four days, tripled in cost, and then driven car sales down more than 40 percent the month after the program ended. That's because President Palin knows too much about economics to push a plan that stupid. If nothing else (attention, Katie Couric!), one of the papers she reads is the *Wall Street Journal.*

President Palin wouldn't have called Afghanistan a "war of necessity" and the "front line in the war on terror," and then announce nine months later she still didn't have a "strategery" to win it. The fact that her own son was in the military would probably have been enough to persuade her against adopting an Obama-style, Hamlet-like state of paralysis. You might agree or disagree with her policy—and quite frankly, I don't know what her policy toward Afghanistan would have been—but once she announced it, nobody would be sitting around wondering what the hell it was.

And one thing's for sure: her strategy wouldn't have been Obama's "Surrender Surge." Sending more troops but announcing you're going to start withdrawing them in eighteen months is, well, bizarre. Obama's "let's send 30,000 more troops, but tell them not to bother to unpack" plan would have been viewed as sheer idiocy if Palin had proposed it. But a President Palin never would.

And when a cop and a professor got into an altercation on a front porch in Cambridge, the sentence in President Palin's speech after, "I don't know all the facts" would have been, "So I'm not going to comment." Not President Obama's "the Cambridge police acted stupidly."

Oh—and care to guess how many photos there would be of President Palin bowing like a doorman to the leaders of Saudi Arabia, Japan, and (believe it or not) to the mayor of Tampa, Florida?

President Palin wouldn't have reached the Oval Office with the support of the child-prostitution enablers at ACORN, and she sure as hell wouldn't have pleaded ignorance about the group receiving millions in government money. (Obama: "I didn't even know that ACORN was getting a whole lot of federal money.")

President Palin never would have given British Prime Minister Gordon Brown an insulting "presidential gift" of twenty-five DVDs that don't even work on British DVD players.

And if Sarah Palin had loaded up Todd and the snow machine onto Air Force One and spent millions in Copenhagen pitching her hometown for the Olympics, her town wouldn't have *come in last* in the vote. She would have been too smart to make the trip in the first place.

Now, I will admit fans of President Obama may contest every one of these points. And some more honest O-bots might concede the facts (kind of hard not to), but reject the argument. "Harvard-educated Barack Obama," they might insist, "is still far more intelligent than Sarah Palin."

And they might be right in a Joe Biden, "I have a much higher IQ than you" sort of way. But I'll point out that Palin is at least as credible at the national level as former Democratic presidential candidates Al Gore or John Kerry. She's just not treated that way.

She Who Laughs Last . . .

Let's be fair: Obama has screwed up repeatedly as president, in part because, as he said on *60 Minutes*, "This is hard." No kidding, Mr. President. Being president actually does involve a little more heavy lifting than serving in the Illinois state legislature.

But c'mon, O-bots, you've got to admit another reason he's struggled is that he had zero executive experience, had never run a town or anything more complicated than a voter registration drive, had never taken on corruption (and in Chicago, I suspect it wasn't too hard to find), and had never been in any tough political fights where he took bold stands and defended them against all comers.

Sarah Palin did all those things before being nominated for Veep. And I think she still wasn't a particularly impressive candidate, though I imagine she would have been after four more years of experience as governor of Alaska, the last two learning the ropes on the national stage.

All of which brings us back to the question I started this chapter with: why do they hate Sarah so?

Love Letter from the Left

"Alaskan hillbillies have been transplanted into the world of Washington politics."

—John Doyle, writer for Canada's *Globe and Mail*, on the Palins

Entire books have been written on the subject—literally. Matthew Continetti theorizes that it was always about Obama, and Palin hatred was inspired by fear that she would upset the pre-ordained storyline of the O's ascendency. "When the beast saw Sarah Palin appear out of thin air and captivate the American imagination, it tore her apart. The hate machine whirred and hummed and swung into high gear," Continetti wrote.

Conservative talk host and columnist Hugh Hewitt sees it this way:

> She is the embodiment of the anti-choice, the opposite of every choice that lefty elites have ever made—as to going back home instead of moving to the west coast, having children, having a child with Down's, staying married to one man the whole time, choosing rural or suburban over urban and living a generally conservative lifestyle, working with her hands....That everything she is, is the antithesis of everything that liberal urban elites are, so it's not just enough to say, "I disagree with you"; she has to be repudiated and crushed.

I've asked a lot of liberals why they hate her, and the most frequent answer I get is this: "Because she's so hateable."

For a different take, I asked my mom about Sarah Palin. Her reaction was tepid at best: not really ready to be president, but could be someday. Likes her attitude, not sure it's presidential, but yeah—she's keeping an eye on her. Interested, but not *that* interested. Not a lot of pro-Palin passion from my conservative, evangelical Christian mom.

But when I asked my mom about the Left's treatment of Palin—she went nuclear. Wow. My God-fearing mother didn't actually use any of George Carlin's "seven words you can't say on TV," but she was thinking at least three of them.

Four when I mentioned Keith Olbermann.

My mom sensed what millions of other typical, average, normal Americans picked up on in the assault against Sarah Palin: that the Alaskan governor was a stand-in for my mom. For her values, her attitudes, her place in our national discussion. In the eyes of the Obama elites, what was Sarah Palin's true offense?

She didn't know her place.

Like the rest of us Obama infidels who haven't seen the One True Light, Palin's job is to defer to Obama's greatness, not to (horrors!) mock his community service. (And she was pretty good at that: "I guess a small-town mayor is sort of like a 'community organizer,' except that you have actual responsibilities.")

When Palin began challenging President Obama's healthcare plans on her Facebook page (oooh, that tricky Alaskan—end-running the mainstream media again!), the overwhelming media reaction was, "Who the hell does she think she is?" The Kool-Aid kids on the pundit couches all but ignored the substance of her comments and attacked her merely for asking the questions.

My mom knew just how Sarah felt.

Palin was asking questions about how to pay for a multi-trillion dollar government program, about how Obama and the Democrats planned to control costs without rationing. She wanted to debate whether or not Americans were ready to join those European countries that deny older folks treatment that a government panel decides isn't cost efficient. Without such treatment, these older patients die. Hmmm.... A "panel" that denies people treatment, resulting in their "death." If only someone could come up with a pithy, catchy way to describe that kind of policy...

Shortly after being mocked for her "death panels" comment, a federal panel overseeing medical treatment issued a recommendation against routine mammograms for women under fifty. A lot of women got the message, especially those who had survived breast cancer discovered by mammograms while in their forties: Palin had been right all along.

But being right is not an acceptable excuse for opposing the Obama agenda. The more Palin prospers by noting the Emperor's lack of clothing, the more angry the political and media establishment becomes. She's keeping alive a conversation they want to end.

The treatment of Sarah Palin by Obama supporters, media elites, and the Hollywood Left is the model for their treatment of the entire tea party/townhall/talk radio universe. They're not as vicious to us, because we're not as prominent or as dangerous to them. They're not as open in their attacks on us because they know that eventually a ballot box will be opening at a polling place near you.

But it's the same fundamental premise: Barack Obama supporters mocking Sarah Palin's experience. Geniuses who blew nearly a trillion dollars on a useless stimulus package calling her stupid. 9/11 truthers accusing Palin of being a nut. Defenders of Roman Polanski making jokes about her parenting skills. She's the stand-in for millions of typical Americans, having the anger and ignorance of the Obama elites dumped upon her in our stead.

So why don't we follow her example and fight back? There's no reason we can't do what Palin's been doing on Facebook, too. We can ask establishment politicians the obvious questions and note the commonsense problems with their plans.

It's not going to be a fair fight. The media are in the tank. The Left will insult you while avoiding your arguments. But if you're going to get trashed anyway—why not grab your "Just Say No to Socialism" sign and head for the nearest townhall meeting?

That's the lesson normal Americans learned from the treatment of Sarah Palin. They're not likely to forget it soon, either.

Once again, I say all this as someone who is at best a mild Sarah Palin fan—I like a dollop of egghead mixed in with the populism. Then again, I'm one of the few people who still has a "Pete DuPont for President" button, so what do I know?

Like some other conservatives, I'm annoyed that Palin bailed on her job as governor—though I completely understand why. Her opponents point to the money she made from her book deal, and I'm sure that was a factor. But the investigations of her office were partisan, bogus, and unending; by stepping down, she probably saved Alaskan taxpayers hundreds of thousands of dollars. Will it hurt her chances for a future run? Absolutely not. It's far better to be a celebrity than a seasoned politician. Just ask half-term senator Barack Obama.

In fact, I predict Sarah Palin won't run for office again if her media career is a success. Why should she? Being president is hard. People pick on you all the time. It doesn't pay particularly well, and you can't really get much done.

Being a celebrity, on the other hand, is a blast. You get cheered all the time, you make the big bucks, and when you talk about an issue, people actually care and get involved. You can send mediocre books to the top of the bestseller list. (If you're reading this, Oprah, I LOVE your show!)

Seriously, who would you rather be in today's America: Obama or Oprah?

If Sarah Palin is smart, she's already figured that out.

And yes, my O-bot friends, she is.

IT DOESN'T MATTER WHAT THIS SIGN SAYS YOU'LL CALL IT RACISM ANYWAY!

Chapter Ten

We Are All Racists Now

"I would ask that you tell Nancy Pelosi, I'm one of those ugly mobsters. I'm not a racist. I'm an American and I'm sick and tired of sitting here every time something goes wrong with the president's plan, we are all racists. Well guess what? If he can call me a racist, more power to him, but he's lying."

—Ron Harwell, a citizen attending his local
congressional townhall meeting in Tennessee

These days, all of us are racists.

You, me, my evangelical Christian Mom—like I said in chapter three, the O-bots have given you a choice: you're either with the plan or in the Klan.

Which is why I'm with Ron Harwell. Go ahead—call me a racist.

In fact, I'm not going to wait for you to do it. I'll say it right up front: *of course* I'm a racist. A sheet-wearing, cross-burning, goose-stepping, lynch-mobbing member of the Aryan Nations, dreaming of the day when the Master Race rises once again to claim the throne of our blond-haired, blue-eyed manifest destiny!

Which is just another way of saying I *didn't* vote for Barack Obama.

And it's not just me. About 200 million other voting-age Americans didn't turn out for Obama, either. Does it matter that some of my fellow "racists"—people who voted for McCain, a third-party candidate, or didn't vote at all—are black, Hispanic, gay, or even all three?

Nope. The O-bots don't do triangulation. There is no third way.

Obama is a living political Rorschach test. He always has been. An unknown state senator gives a single speech at the 2004 Democratic National Convention and instantly becomes a competitive national candidate? This doesn't happen to Illinois legislator Bill O'Bannion or Bob Olsen.

It's simply an undeniable fact that race opened the door to the presidency for Obama. His intelligence, hard work, smart campaigning—and his understanding of the powerful appeal for the vast majority of Americans of voting for a black man—closed the deal.

It's hardly a surprise, therefore, that the race-obsessed Left would assume that everyone else embraces identity politics, too. They simply can't imagine Americans who don't see the world through the prism of race. And the Left is so arrogant they simply can't imagine any legitimate reason why anyone would vote against them.

So why didn't Obama get my vote? Was it race?

It certainly wasn't because I'm a McCain man. I spent most of the Bush administration beating the ideological snot out of McCain over issues like amnesty for illegal immigrants, his opposition to tax cuts, and his unwillingness to fight for conservative judges. During the 2008 GOP primary, I started a website called mydearjohnletter.com for people like me who supported McCain in 2000 but, after watching him pander to the *New York Times* editorial board for eight years, had no desire to do so ever again.

So, theoretically, my vote was up for grabs in the general election of 2008. I admit that the chances I would vote for the most liberal major-party candidate since LBJ were slim, but it was possible. The fact is, I didn't reject Obama based on his ideology, or his lack of experience, or his policy proposals. As a candidate, Barack Obama never made it that far with me. I couldn't vote for him under any circumstances, even if he'd been a Reaganite conservative with a plan to balance the budget in one pocket and a "hot chicks for middle-aged talk hosts" proposal in the other.

And to be brutally honest, in the end it *was* all about race with me.

You see, as a voter, I have one very simple rule: I never vote for any candidate who spent twenty years in a racist, anti-Semitic, anti-American church. Period.

You spend two decades in the Church of the Klan, or Louis Farrakhan's Anti-Semite Assembly, or under the pastorage of a "mentor" like the Reverend Jeremiah Wright, and you lose my vote. Donate tens of thousands of dollars to such a racist anti-Semite, as Obama did, and there's no way I can support you.

It's not partisan. It's principle. And for upholding this principle—no supporters of racist whackjobs get my support for president—I have been declared a bigot by the elitist Left. In the upside down world of the Obama Nation, people who spend a lifetime following Reverend Wright *aren't* racists. But people who show up at a rally to oppose single-payer healthcare *are*.

If that's the standard the mainstream media and liberal "thinkers" are going to use to accuse American citizens of racism, then hell yes, I'm a racist. And I'll take a mob of "reactionary racists" over the cheering congregation of Jeremiah "God Damn America!" Wright's church any time.

"Mom, Why Do My Pillow Cases Have Eye-Holes?"

When I found out—from a former President of the United States, no less—that my very own mother was, in fact, part of America's white supremacist movement, I was shocked and stunned. And you know who was even more surprised? My mom.

After all, she's had to confront racism face to face. After growing up in the multiracial mixing bowl of Los Angeles, Pat Graham followed her husband Simon to Columbia, South Carolina, just as desegregation was fully taking effect. Unlike most of the MSNBC big mouths screaming about "racist teabaggers," my mom actually had to deal with racism head on.

In Columbia, my mom enrolled me in the local elementary school during the first year of desegregation, so I was in the first class of white students to attend this previously all-black school. When my family could afford to move out of our little duplex and into a real house in the country later that year, my mom picked me up at school after my last day in this once-segregated classroom. When she did, the teacher thanked my mother for not pulling me out of the school sooner.

My mom was confused. "Why would I do that?"

"All the other white parents pulled their kids out right away. Your son has been the only white child in my class for weeks. Didn't he tell you?"

Apparently I hadn't, probably because I hadn't noticed. But it wouldn't have mattered anyway. My parents sent me to school to get an education. They didn't care what the kids I sat next to looked like.

We relocated to rural Lexington County, a place where calling someone a racist wasn't just a cheap debate tactic. In fact, depending on who you were speaking to, it wasn't necessarily even an insult. Vernon King—then the head of the South Carolina Ku Klux Klan—lived around the corner from us. I rode the school bus with his sons. The handful of local KKK clowns staged occasional cross burnings and public declarations of inbred stupidity.

But Pat and Simon Graham would have none of it. Their evangelical faith reminded them that man looked upon the outward appearance but God looked upon the heart, and they tried to follow His example. They were both active in multiracial Christian ministries like Full Gospel Businessmen's Fellowship and Women's Aglow. My mom participated in targeted outreach to welcome black Christians into common worship.

At home, they wouldn't allow racist language, didn't tolerate racist attitudes, and joined my sister and me in mocking the handful of racist nitwits who gave our community a bad name.

So imagine her surprise to discover that, in the era of Obama, she had unknowingly joined the same Klansmen we used to mock from our front porch. From LBJ to George W. Bush, my mom had been an open-hearted church lady actively working to bridge the racial divide. Then President Obama is elected and—voila! Pat "Grand Dragon" Graham.

What happened?

Love Letter from the Left

"It was a Klan rally minus the bedsheets and torches."

—William Rivers Pitt, former spokesman for Democratic congressman Dennis Kucinich, on the 9/12 tea party in Washington, D.C.

Politics.

As I mentioned earlier in this book, calling a talk show host or political activist names is no big deal. We're used to it, particularly the charge of "racism." It used to bother me, but now it's lost all its power because it's used too spuriously and too often.

When I worked at WBT-AM in Charlotte, North Carolina, for example, I was denounced for opposing racial quotas in the city's magnet schools. Dedicated students who wanted to attend special math-focused public schools were being turned away based on their race. If the school was deemed "too black"—that is, the proportion of black students was higher than the government allowed under racial quotas—then desks were left empty rather than giving the space to black students trying to escape their lousy, local public school. I thought this was an outrage. You know what I got called for fighting to get black students into better schools?

"Racist."

And that sure wasn't the only time. When a group of black ministers began pushing for "black-only" public schools under the theory that black students learn differently from white ones, I was enraged. I pointed out that this was the same theory George Wallace used to support segregation in the 1950s. What did supporters of these race-based schools call me?

"Racist."

When union stooges attacked standardized testing for teachers or police officers because, they claimed, it wasn't fair to black and Hispanic applicants, I pointed out how insulting their assumption was. I completely rejected the idea that people's skin color made them too dumb to take the same tests as everyone else. What was the reaction to my claim that intelligence is NOT race-based?

"Racist!"

So for me, getting called racist is just part of the job. The fact that the people making these charges want the government to treat people differently *based on their race* makes it that much more entertaining.

But for typical Americans who've never been active in politics, being called a racist is both serious and scary. It's the rhetorical equivalent of being charged with rape. Even when proven untrue, the charge itself is damaging to your character.

White Americans—or if you prefer, "persons of pallor"—have seen the charge of racism wreck entire careers. And not just in politics. We've seen co-workers disciplined or fired over allegations of racism that were, at best, questionable and sometimes out-and-out laughable.

One classic example was in 2005 when the mayor of Columbus, Georgia, was forced to write an apology to an irate activist offended by the behavior of some police officers at a civil rights march. What was the offensive behavior? They were eating bananas.

Aha! And why were the cops eating bananas? To quote from Mayor Poydasheff's apology, "The officers needed some nutrition after standing long hours on the street, and they particularly needed the potassium available in bananas and some other fruits. Accordingly, they were given bananas along with some drinking water."

Why apologize? Why didn't the mayor just tell this moron to get a life? Because her charge against him wasn't "corruption" or "incompetence" or even "nutritional malfeasance." It was "racism." Once that poisonous element is added to any composition, the entire mixture becomes toxic. As stupid as this charge was, it still carried the day.

That's the power of the race card. And it's not just fear that creates this power; it's the anger against racial injustice most white Americans share. Racism is a particularly brutal and ugly form of stupidity. The treatment of black Americans in the past shocks and hurts our sensibilities, particularly those of us born after Jim Crow and segregation.

Sometimes I get the sense that liberals think all white people nurture an inner Aryan who longs to be free. They think that hilarious Eddie Murphy bit on *Saturday Night Live* about how white people act when black people aren't around ("What a silly Negro!") is grounded in truth.

Sorry, but you've got it backward. If anything, most white Americans second-guess themselves constantly, looking for signs of latent racism or unintended bigotry. It's easy to mock white people who invoke the "some of my best friends are black" defense, but however ham-fisted the effort, the speaker is trying to show that he's actively thinking about racial issues in his own life. He's genuinely concerned about the impact of his own words and deeds.

Of course there are still racist morons among us. (Al Sharpton and Jesse Jackson haven't gone anywhere, have they?) But there's something truly bizarre when the same America where a coalition of white, Hispanic, and black voters proudly elected Barack Obama president is forced to listen as Attorney General Eric Holder calls them "a nation of cowards" when it comes to race.

This from the same attorney general who supported the fire department in New Haven, Connecticut, for refusing promotions to qualified white and Hispanic firefighters purely based on their race. The same Holder who mysteriously dropped a federal case against nightstick-wielding members of the New Black Panther Party caught on videotape at polling places, yelling racial epithets at would-be voters. Even after the Justice Department had effectively won the case, Holder still dropped it.

Thanks, Captain Courage!

Which is why this attack on typical Americans like my mom as "white supremacists" is so maddening—maddening, ignorant, and unfair.

Some of My Best Friends Are Tea Partiers

During the height of the tea party protests in 2009, I was invited to appear on the *Dr. Phil* show to play the "designated white guy"—or, as I later told the Reverend Al Sharpton, the "Caucasian of Designation." The topic of the show was "What No One Wants to Admit: Racism and Racial Stereotypes." The guest panel was a rainbow coalition of ethnicities assigned to discuss the ugly role of racism in American society. And what was the very first example they came up with?

The tea party protesters.

"Of course it's racist," growled comedian Paul Mooney, wearing a sequined shirt that read, "Black Man. Please Don't Shoot." He added, "[The protesters] can't stand a black man in the White House."

Not to be outdone, University of Southern California professor of sociology Amon Emeka raised the chilling specter of an insurrection among these racists. "And where was the first tea party? In

Boston," he noted ominously. "Remember that the point of the original Boston Tea party was to overthrow the government. Is that what they want to do, overthrow the Obama administration?"

A murmur went through the studio audience. "Yeah, what are those tea party weirdos up to?" they seemed to be asking. And suddenly, every eye turned to me. It seemed more than a few were thinking, "How 'bout it, angry racist white guy? Or should we say, 'Homegrown terrorist radical!'" Having personally organized a tea party on Boston Harbor—complete with folks in colonial garb tossing tea chests into the harbor—this wasn't an entirely comfortable moment for me. So I decided to save that bit of my biography for a future *Dr. Phil* appearance.

I couldn't help noticing the irony of the situation. The show's premise that day was that it was stupid and wrong to make assumptions about people based on the group they're in; that we should overlook stereotypes and try to understand the individual; and most of all, that it's wrong to take the bad actions of a single person and extrapolate them to impugn the character of an entire group.

And who is the most guilty of that, these smug liberals asked on national television? Why, those crazy racist teabaggers, of course! They're all a bunch of violent bigots—every one of 'em! You see the sign that one guy had comparing Obama to Hitler? That's what they're all like, those goose-stepping white supremacists!

Isn't it great when liberals stand up against the scourge of stereotyping?

When it was my turn to speak, I pointed out that tea party protests were hardly new—I organized my first one as a political flak in 1994. Professor Emeka was genuinely surprised. He really thought the tea parties were some dangerous new development, perhaps linked to the militia movement, survivalist cults, or—worst case scenario—the *Glenn Beck* show. This from a college professor whose purported area of expertise is U.S. politics and society?

As we talked, it became increasingly clear that, while he was a pleasant, intelligent guy, Professor Emeka knew virtually nothing about the history of American conservatism or any of the issues that motivated the Obama-era protests. He couldn't even tell me, "Some of my best friends are tea partiers"—I'm sure he'd never met a single member of the movement he was casually denouncing on national TV as a potential threat to the republic.

Say what you want about the remaining members of the KKK (all six of them), but even those hate-filled, racist buffoons actually *know* some black people. Most of the arrogant celebrities who insult typical Americans like my mom can't even say that. Here, for example, is our good friend Janeane Garofalo, appearing on *Real Time with Bill Maher*:

> It's obvious to anybody who has eyes in this country that tea-baggers, the 9/12ers, these separatist groups that pretend that it's about policy—they are clearly white-identity movements. They're clearly white power movements. What they don't like about the president is that he's black—or half-black—and they, what also is shocking is that people keep pretending that that's not really the case with these people.
>
> I'm not talking about people that do have problems with his policies, that's fine. But these people, who are also being led by the Glenn Becks, the Michele Bachmanns, the Rush Limbaughs, whomever, they are no different than any other white identity movement that's part of our history.
>
> This has been going on since the founding of this country that white power movements have tried to establish themselves and hold onto power.

Love Letter from the Left

"Do you remember tea baggers? It was just so much easier when we could just call them racists."

—Janeane Garofalo

What a stroke of good fortune for Garofalo that this "white power" activity at tea parties and townhalls is "obvious to anyone who has eyes." If it weren't, she might be forced to offer some actual evidence substantiating her vicious and idiotic statement. Even worse, those tea party meanies "keep pretending" they're not actually white supremacists. They come up with phony "policy issues" about healthcare, debt, and government spending. How bogus is that? Ooooooh, that makes Janeane SOOOOOO mad!

And so she calls them white supremacists on national TV, offers no proof whatsoever, and...nothing. That should be strange. That should get folks upset. It doesn't, and that's a problem.

Let's say, for example, I were going to call Janeane an anti-Semite on national TV. Pretty big deal, right? I'd feel some need to have some evidence to back that up. I'd feel pressure to have my facts straight before making such a powerful and destructive accusation.

Not Ms. Garofalo. She simply announces that millions of average Americans are part of the "white power movement"— and then she calls it a day. And nobody ever challenged her. Not a single CNN reporter asked her to substantiate her accusation. (You'd think CNN could find time to do it, since they fact checked a *Saturday Night Live* skit poking fun at their Dear

Leader, the Great and Wondrous O.) To Garofalo, the MSM, and to so many other O-bots, the racism charge is self-evident.

Barack, Meet Jesse

Like most typical Americans, it never occurred to my mom that attending a rally opposing government-run healthcare and massive government debt had anything to do with race. My mom thought it was about math. Since when is a $14 trillion national debt just the white man's burden?

The record debt President Obama racked up is going to be paid back by Americans of all races, creeds, and colors. So given that we're all stuck together on the taxpayer *Titanic*, how does it make you a racist to yell out, "Watch out for the iceberg!"

(Unless it's because icebergs are all . . . *white*? And I suppose it's a coincidence that they're ice "bergs?" What, was "Ice-steins" already taken, you anti-Semitic hatemongers?)

I've attended a dozen taxpayer protests, I've taken literally a thousand phone calls about the lousy job the Obama administration's done on the stimulus, spending, debt, healthcare—and not one of them has ever involved a policy issue related to race. Not one.

And yet, I'd be willing to bet there hasn't been a single 24-hour news cycle since President Obama took office in which he or one of his supporters hasn't played the race card. Yes, Obama has magnanimously assured us that it's possible to disagree with him on policy without being racist. But if his supporters agree that it's possible, they consider it highly unlikely.

Race is to Obama liberals what marijuana is to libertarians. Here's what I mean: ever notice how libertarians *always* talk about marijuana? It doesn't matter what subject they start with—healthcare, taxes, wearing white after Labor Day—their argument always ends the same way: "...and that's why we need to legalize pot!"

The O-bots are the same way with race. In the Obama era, every policy debate is a debate on race. Opposition to liberal proposals isn't about governance, it's a revelation of the inherent racism of the American character. Here are just a few examples:

- Did you think the stimulus plan sucked? "Opposition to the federal stimulus package by southern GOP governors is a slap in the face of African-Americans."
  —Democratic congressman James Clyburn.
- Hate the Obama healthcare scheme? "Opposition To Obama/Health Care Reform Racist!"
  —*Huffington Post* and Media Matters blogger Oliver Willis
- Show up at a tea party? Well, liberals are willing to admit it's at least statistically possible you're not a racist—but you probably are, anyway. From MSNBC:

  Chris Matthews: Put 100 of these people [tea party attendees] in a room. Strap them into gurneys. Inject them with sodium pentathol. How many of them would say, "I don't like the idea of having a black president"? What percentage?
  Atlanta-Journal Constitution columnist Cynthia Tucker: Oh, I'm just guessing. This is just off the cuff. I think 45 to 65 percent of the people who appear at these groups are people who

will never be comfortable with the idea of a
black president.

How bad is it? One of my regular radio show callers, a black man
who's a huge Obama supporter, called my show to complain that
I never had anything positive to say about the president. He suggested that it was because of race. I acknowledged that Obama
hadn't done much I liked, but I reminded the caller that a few
months earlier I had supported the president's decision to order
the shooting of some Somali pirates who were holding an American hostage.

After pondering this for a moment, the caller retorted (I'm par-
aphrasing here), "You only liked it because the pirates who got
shot were black!"

You can't win.

And typical Americans have figured that out. The game is fixed
and everyone knows it. It's not the race card, it's the *race coin*:
heads, you're a racist; tails, you're a bigot.

That's why Ron Harwell of Tennessee briefly became a TV
celebrity after making the comment that opened this chapter.
And that's why one of the most popular signs at the tea party
rallies reads, "It Doesn't Matter What My Sign Says, You'll Still
Call It Racist."

And it's not just white people. Lloyd Marcus, a black conservative who has attended several tea parties, reported this experience:

> I was interviewed on CNN. During the pre-interview by the
> young black producer over the phone, he asked me, "Is there
> any part of Obama's healthcare plan you like"? I replied,
> "No." He was stunned. With great shock and disbelief in his

voice, the producer repeated my reply with a loud "NO?"
Then he abruptly said, "I'll call you back."

I already mentioned a similar case of another black dissident,
Kenneth Gladney, who was at a St. Louis townhall meeting selling "Don't Tread On Me" flags to opponents of ObamaCare. A
couple SEIU thugs roughed him up on camera. One union
knuckle dragger wanted to know "What kind of 'N' are you [as
Gladney put it] giving this stuff away around here?" Gladney
ended up in the hospital.

Even Alabama congressman Artur Davis, a member of the
Congressional Black Caucus and loyal Democrat, had to learn
the hard way. When he voted against ObamaCare, Jesse Jackson
attacked, exclaiming, "You can't vote against health care and call
yourself a black man."

Voting against Barack can actually knock the black out of you?
That's not playing the race card, that's swinging the race tire iron.
If a black Democratic congressman gets a beatdown like this,
everyone else who opposes Obama is obviously doomed.

Congressman Davis, showing more class in a moment than
Jackson's shown in a lifetime, graciously responded by saying,
"The best way to honor Reverend Jackson's legacy is to decline
to engage in an argument with him that begins and ends in race."

Classy, but completely wrong. Jesse Jackson's *entire existence*
begins and ends with race. Take him out to dinner, and over cock-
tails he lectures you for ordering a white Russian. He storms
away during dessert because you didn't eat the black forest cake.

Many Americans, including quite a few who didn't vote for
Barack, hoped that an Obama presidency would reject Jack-
son/Sharpton-style race baiting and divisive opportunism.

Unfortunately, that hasn't been the case—not by a long shot.

"You Lie!"

A revealing racial moment occurred in August 2009, about eight months into the Obama administration. During the heat of the healthcare debate, President Obama addressed a joint session of Congress to push for his healthcare "reform." During a contentious speech in which the president accused his opponents of lying and "playing games," he said that claims that his health plan would cover illegal immigrants were "not true. They are false."

Congressman Joe Wilson blurted out, "You lie!"

Wilson was actually right—illegals would have received health coverage, because the bill did not require anyone to show proof of legal residence. The White House implicitly admitted this two days later by asking that such a requirement be added to the bill.

Still, what Wilson did was wrong. It was crass, and it was rude. Wilson (who happens to be my mom's congressman—coincidence . . . or something more?) apologized to President Obama the night of his outburst, and again the next morning. Obama accepted the apology and said, "We have to get to the point where we can have a conversation about big, important issues that matter to the American people without vitriol, without name-calling, without the assumption of the worst of other people's motives."

Team Obama then promptly began making assumptions about Wilson's motives.

New York Times columnist Maureen Dowd—the Cosmo girl of political columnists—said of Wilson's exclamation, "What I heard was an unspoken word in the air: You lie, *boy*!"

Her hallucination was capably rebutted by pundit and former psychiatrist Charles Krauthammer: "In my previous profession, I saw many people who heard words that weren't said. They were called 'patients.' Many were helped with medication."

Dowd wasn't alone, however. It seemed the entire Left lined up to declare Joe Wilson a racist—and make sure everyone else did it, too. When a black congresswoman from Maryland declined to call Wilson a bigot on his show, MSNBC host Chris Matthews stopped the interview, re-asked the question, and then tried to browbeat her into uttering the "R" word.

A few days after Joe Wilson's outburst, a million Americans rallied against big government at the 9/12 tea party in D.C. Even though Wilson didn't participate in the event in any way, network broadcasts ran "news" stories linking his shout to the racism they claimed was motivating the rally. Democratic congresswoman Maxine Waters, for example, implied that protestors' use of the phrase "ObamaCare" was racist. On a podcast of liberal talk host Bill Press, she also asked the media to look into the minds of protesters. "I want those people talked to," she declared. "I want them interviewed. I want the journalists to be all over those rallies and those marches of the Birthers and the tea baggers—let's find out what they think."

Really, Maxine, you can't figure that out on your own? The huge "No More Big Government!" signs they're waving aren't a clue?

Other House Democrats joined Waters in passing a resolution condemning Wilson for refusing to apologize a second time. Wilson argued that the president had accepted his apology, and as far as he was concerned that was that. But that wasn't good enough for Speaker Pelosi and the Democrats. Democratic congressman Hank Johnson claimed that if Congress failed to rebuke Wilson, "I guess we'll probably have folks putting on white hoods and white uniforms again, riding through the countryside intimidating people."

Huh? "Putting on white hoods?" Yep, that's what the man said. Shouting at the president today; burning giant crosses alongside your cousin/wife tomorrow.

Sound crazy to you? Well, a certain former Democratic president managed to out-crazy even that. Attributing the "overwhelming portion" of the "animosity" toward Obama to racist resentment against a black man, Jimmy Carter warned of "a belief among many white people, not just in the South but around the country, that African-Americans are not qualified to lead this great country. It's an abominable circumstance and grieves me and concerns me very deeply."

Notice that Carter didn't even bother to limit his accusation of racism to talk radio listeners or tea partiers, as lefties usually do. Instead, it was a near-blanket condemnation of whites. Dissent, which liberals declared "the highest form of patriotism" during the Bush years, was now rejected as the lowest form of racism. In the Obama era, all dissent is mere cover for white supremacist tendencies.

And so Jimmy Carter didn't care how many signs about health-care and home mortgages appeared at the townhalls or tea parties. Carter just knows that the people are "overwhelmingly" motivated by race, that "many white people" are bigots.

Speaking of windows into the mind, Carter may be an idiot to most Americans, but it turns out he was speaking for a significant number of liberals. According to a Rasmussen Reports poll, 12 percent of American voters "believe that most opponents of President Obama's health care reform plan are racist." Unfortunately—and this explains why more and more average Americans like liberals less and less—22 percent of Democrats say most of the opposition to Obama's plan comes from racists, and another 39 percent are not sure.

In other words, 61 percent of Democrats either think criticizing Obama makes you a Klansman or they're not sure. Then again, what did we expect from those tolerant, non-judgmental liberals in the first place?

The Obama elites are so certain you're racist that they'll even label you a bigot for denying your alleged bigotry. I found this out during the Joe Wilson kerfuffle, when I used my radio show to rebut the constant slurs that talk radio listeners are all racists. After the show, a liberal co-worker told me, "You know, Michael, when I hear you and other conservatives going on and on about charges of 'racism,' I have to tell you—I think thou dost protest too much. Sounds like there's something there to me."

When I pointed out that we conservatives were minding our own business when this "bigotry" barrage came crashing in from the Left, she simply repeated the charge. When I asked her to name a single racist action related to the healthcare debate or Obama policy from anyone this side of Lyndon LaRouche—she repeated it again.

"I don't know, Michael. It sounds like the guy who goes around protesting gay bars because he can't come out of the closet."

"But I'm not out looking for people to call me racist," I replied. "I just turn on my TV and there they are."

She shrugged. "All I'm saying is, when there's smoke . . ." And then she walked away.

Smoke? WHAT smoke? Smoking gun? Smoking jacket? Smoke 'em if you got 'em? Show me some racist smoke!

Silence. The charge of racism has been made, and the verdict is both immediate and final.

Team Obama knows the power of this rhetorical dynamite. It knows how to use it to push through far-Left policies most Americans oppose. The fact is, most Americans would even rather be called socialists than racists. If they had to choose between the two, they'd break out the hammer and sickle every time.

So what can typical Americans do who have sincere concerns about the Obama elite's agenda? You have three choices:

You can outwardly agree with the O-bots, which means you're a closet racist.

You can voice your concerns, get called a racist, refuse to respond, and your silence will prove that you are, in fact, a racist.

Or you can fight back. You can make rational arguments, you can point out the racist charge is both vicious and unfounded. You can demand proof, and confront the liberal accusers with the demonstrable racism of their own actions and policies.

And fighting back will prove to liberals that you are, without a doubt, the biggest racist of all.

Chapter Eleven

The Government Is Made for Porn

I have seen the future of America under ObamaCare, and it's sitting behind a government computer surfing porn.

The *Washington Times* broke the story in September 2009: so many government workers at the National Science Foundation (NSF, not to be confused with NSFW) were conducting (ahem) freelance research on human reproduction that the Inspector General's Office was swamped. It had to pull people from their real jobs—checking grant applications to the $6 billion agency for fraud—and put them on dirty website duty.

The bad news? "We anticipate a significant decline in investigative recoveries and prosecutions in coming years as a direct result," the IG reported.

The good news? Office morale has never been higher! You have to practically force some of these guys to go home at night.

One senior NSF executive spent 331 days surfing porn on his government computer, sometimes even chatting online with overseas porn workers. How could he get away it for nearly a year? Because he doesn't "work." He has a government job. And as anyone can tell you, there's a world of difference.

You want to know the real divide between typical America and the Obama Nation? My mom has never in her life said the sentence, "You know, this would work a lot better if the government were doing it." Team Obama, on the other hand, approaches every problem with precisely that attitude.

Pundits and academics can debate the merits of the Austrian School vs. Keynesian economics until the cows come to their marginal utilization point, but for regular folks who attend tea parties, it comes down to a simple truth: the government fouls up everything it does. U.S. soldiers surrounded by the stupidity of the Army bureaucracy some seventy years ago even invented an acronym for it: SNAFU.

Situation Normal. All F... Well, let's say, "not working very well."

And while Harry Reid and Nancy Pelosi like talking about "expanding healthcare for all" or "leading the way on global warming," typical talk radio listeners have decoded that message: more government workers screwing up more of your life.

Forget liberal vs. conservative, Republican vs. Democrat, talk radio vs. NPR. Millions of Americans find the notion of the government controlling their healthcare or monitoring their thermostats or running a car company absolutely insane. Not because they've read Ayn Rand, but because they've been to the post office. Who wants their doctor's office to become more like that—

anyone? Who wants their business practices governed by the federal equivalent of their local school board—you?

Have you ever walked into a private-sector business, looked around at a group of hard-working, successful employees and said, "Wow—this place is humming along like the National Science Foundation! By the way, anyone checked out Miss January today?"

This may surprise Team Obama, but when typical Americans use the phrase "good enough for government work," it's not a compliment.

Media mockers of the tea partiers have focused like a laser beam on the protest signs referencing socialism, misreading them as ideological. "What socialism?" detractors ask. But they're missing the point. Sure, there are some "Reagan Capitalism vs. The Evil Empire" types protesting Obama policies. (I'm proud to be one of them.) Our numbers are dwarfed, however, by protesters who read "socialism" as "government-run," which is why every "Obama = Socialist" sign is typically surrounded by a dozen more direct messages like, "Hands Off My Healthcare" and "Obama-Care: If It's Not Good Enough For His Kids, It's Not Good Enough For Mine."

Everyone knows that "government-run" is Washington-ese for "it sucks." During the healthcare debate, Republican senators Tom Coburn and Charles Grassley each proposed in their own committees that if a public option passed, members of the White House and Congress would be required to sign up for it. "I can think of no better way to ensure that the public option is responsive to our citizens then by having the politicians in charge... enrolled in the program," Coburn said.

The liberal leadership in Congress said, "No problem!" Relevant amendments passed both the Finance Committee and the

Health, Education, Labor, and Pensions Committee. But something happened on the way to full Senate approval. The staff of Senate leadership offices and committees—the bureaucrats with the most pull—were suddenly exempted from the requirement.

It was yet another tacit admission that the tea party crowd was right: nobody wants his healthcare run by the government.

No Sale on "Free" Healthcare

On Christmas Eve 2009, Senate Democrats tried to shove ObamaCare down America's throats by the slimmest possible margin, approving the bill after rushing through several procedural votes in the wee hours of the morning. Yet polls showed just 40 percent of Americans supported the "reform," even though President Obama repeatedly assured the American people his plan would save money for everyone—families, businesses, and the government.

Think about that for a moment: politicians are trying to give away "free" healthcare, and they can't get a majority of people to take it? That's incredible. It's like a smokin' hot woman walking into a bar on a Friday night offering casual sex, and having more than half the drunks look her over and say, "Eh, not interested."

But maybe there's a rational explanation for this. Perhaps the American people don't really believe the Democrats' assurances that they can get something for nothing, and that it'll be good. Maybe they understand this isn't "free healthcare" falling from heaven, or delivered by an alien race with superior technology, or even by the U.S. Marines. Eventually, at some point, there's going to be a unionized employee from a government "Department of You Have to Stand in My Line" deciding when—or even if—you get to see a doctor.

Americans who work in the private sector don't trust the government to do its job. And if you know any government workers, most of them will tell you they think the public sector sucks, too.

That's one reason why, as the prospect of government-run healthcare became more real, support for it plunged. In 2007, 28 percent of Americans told Gallup they didn't believe it was the government's responsibility to provide healthcare for all. Less than two years later, when it became clear Team Obama was going to use actual government workers to do just that, the number jumped to 50 percent. And that huge swing can't be blamed on current events, or some freak Katrina-like healthcare disaster.

All it took was typical Americans thinking about what it will be like when the lady screwing up your car registration at the end of a four-hour line becomes the lady screwing up your medical records at the end of an even longer line.

No, not all government workers are incompetent. But all government workers work *for the government*; that is, they're in an environment where mediocrity is considered good enough, and where there are no consequences for being lousy at your job.

This brings us back to the government porn kings of the NSF. According to the *Washington Times*, one of those guys was caught with "hundreds of pictures, videos and even PowerPoint slide shows containing pornography." When asked if he had done any actual work the day he downloaded the porn, the employee responded, "Um, I can't remember."

Please allow me to refresh your memory, my future Director of the Office of Mammogram Avoidance. It was the day you showed up at your cushy government gig, did absolutely nothing of any value for eight hours, and got a generous check from the taxpayers for your trouble.

In other words, *every* day.

Government porn, it turns out, is nothing new. I was hosting a radio talk show in Cincinnati in 2002 when the story broke of a city attorney who'd been spending up to eight hours a day cruising the naughtier corners of the porn-iverse. In fact, on some days the guy put in "porn overtime," spending more taxpayer time on porn sites than there were hours in his shift.

After he was caught, his boss argued against firing him. Here's why: despite the fact that he spent hundreds of hours surfing "LustyLawyers.net," he was still the most productive lawyer on the staff. (Pardon the pun.)

When the hardest-working guy in the office spends his days typing with one hand—you know you've got a government job.

In Boston, the subject of inept government hackery really hits home. In the case of the Big Dig, it actually hit the hood of a car. Less than two years after the official opening of the biggest public works project in U.S. history, the $22 billion (and climbing) tunnel had already killed a woman when part of the ceiling fell on her car.

How do you spend $20 billion and still build a tunnel that kills people? You let the government do it. I prefer the good old days, when the government was expected to be corrupt but at least somewhat competent. Back then, if you told the first Mayor Daley you were giving Chicago $20 billion to build a tunnel, he'd make sure you got a really good $10 billion tunnel. Today, you get one you can't even drive through.

The open road isn't much better. Massachusetts toll collectors earn close to $70,000 a year in wages and benefits. For what? Handing out toll tickets and collecting change? Nice work if you can get it—and if you work for the government, you can.

In fact, you can get it without actually *working*. Despite the fact that they work in a phone booth-sized box and never lift anything heavier than a roll of quarters, Massachusetts toll takers have the highest rate of worker's comp claims out of all state employees—including police and firemen.

Then there's the story of the Senior Data Processing Systems Analyst in the Boston Department of Public Works who was allowed to spend six months "working" from home. In the era of telecommuting, that's no big deal, right? Only in this case, her "home" was a beachfront villa in Venezuela.

For six months, on the taxpayer dime, she did her job for a local municipal government from a different *continent*. And why not? I don't blame her for wanting to spend the winter in warmer climates. After all, people take government jobs with the expectation of a light workload, liquid lunches, and the occasional opportunity for low-level graft.

But the "telecommuting from beaches of Venezuela" angle raises entirely new issues. After all, shouldn't city workers who get their drink on during business hours at least have the decency to do so at bars within the Boston city limits? Whatever happened to supporting the local economy?

I say, if Hugo Chavez wants Caracas nightclubs filled with cash-waving government employees, let *him* pay for it.

Love Letter from the Left

"There is a good reason why we have an exemption to the free speech protected by the first amendment, when we say, 'You cannot shout fire in a crowded theater.' And he's doing that every night."

—*Huffington Post* founder Arianna Huffington, supporting the censorship of Glenn Beck

Government workers not doing their jobs cleaning the streets or issuing business licenses is one thing. But can you imagine what will happen if they figure out they could be not doing their jobs from anywhere in the Western hemisphere? We'll never see them again.

You'll be trying to track down the "telecommuting" city employee who lost your sewer payment and erroneously had your water service shut off, and he'll be leaning over a craps table in Nevada shouting, "Come on, seven! Daddy needs a new pair of shoes!"

Do we really want the Service Employees International Union's new motto to be, "What Happens in South America, Stays in South America?"

The Government: Where Accountability Goes to Die

When my mom moved from L.A. to South Carolina in the early 1970s, she worked for the government for a short time. She got a job in the state Department of Revenue pulling in the big bucks: $75 a week. It was lousy pay for a mindless job, but what my mom remembers most about the job was that she was promoted eleven times in five years.

She'd worked her entire life—as a waitress, at a Hughes Tool Company plant in Culver City—and she brought that private sector ethos with her. As a result, she was repeatedly promoted over her fellow longtime government employees. "If you showed any initiative at all, the managers spotted you right away," my mom said. "You really stood out."

When you point out that government workers produce less but still get better benefits than private sector workers, they inevitably reply that it's because they earn less income than in the private sector. And that may have been true back when my mom was in state government. But not anymore.

From the Cato Institute:

> The average federal worker earned $100,178 in wages and benefits in 2004, which compared to $51,876 for the average private-sector worker, according to U.S. Bureau of Economic Analysis data. Looking just at wages, federal workers earned an average $66,558, 56 percent more than the $42,635 earned by the average private worker.
>
> Figure 1 shows that federal compensation has grown more rapidly than private compensation in recent years. Since 1990, average compensation has increased 115 percent in the government and 69 percent in the private sector, while average wages have increased 104 percent in the government and 65 percent in the private sector.

No wonder my pal John Derbyshire at *National Review Online* has taken up the cry "Get a Government Job!" Here's one of his recent postings:

> I keep telling you. Why don't you listen?
>
>> Washington, D.C. has become the favorite area for wealthy young adults, with the nation's highest percentage of 25–34 year-olds making more than $100,000 a year, according to a new analysis.
>
> If you're not working for the feddle gummint either directly (Assistant to Administrative Assistant Grade 3(a) in the U.S. Department of Administrative Assistance) or indirectly

> (lobbying, lawyering, feeding the beast, or living on bailout
> subsidies) you are a loser chump.
>
> Write out 100 times: THE PRIVATE SECTOR IS FOR
> LOSER CHUMPS. Then, go beg a bureaucrat for a job.

Derb is certainly right from the "short-term, self-interest" point of view, but tea partiers are looking further down the road. Somebody has to pay all these government hacks, and it can't be the Federal Department of Hackery Enforcement. For, as every talk listener knows, the government has no money. *We* have money. They take it from us.

When there aren't any "us's" left in the private sector, there won't be any money to feed the government beast. And that's a very real possibility, because government workers don't just earn more than we private-sector chumps do. As Ed Morrissey at HotAir.com reported, since the Left has taken control of Congress and the White House, there are more government workers overall—way more: "In the first six months of [2009], the federal government was adding 10,000 jobs per month, and over the recession had grown the ranks of bureaucrats by 9.8 percent. The private sector, during that same period, shed 7.3 million jobs."

In the worst economy since the Great Depression, while private sector employment was falling about 10 percent, government employment (i.e. "jobs paid for by private taxpayers") were rising by about the same percent.

A December 2009 *USA Today* story contained this nugget:

> When the recession started, the Transportation Department
> had one person earning a salary of $170,000 or more. Eighteen
> months later, 1,690 employees had salaries of $170,000
> or more.... The growth in six-figure salaries has pushed the

average federal worker's pay to $71,206, compared with $40,331 in the private sector.

There is a massive disconnect between the lax demands on government workers and the results-oriented accountability of the private-sector taxpayers who fund them. Full pensions after twenty-five years, full medical benefits after retirement, sick day buybacks—these are standard in the public sector but almost unheard of for the rest of us.

This partly explains why the "quit rate" among federal employees is about a quarter of the private sector rate. It doesn't hurt that only about one in 5,000 non-defense federal workers are fired due to poor performance each year. And that helps explain why the other 4,999 act like such arrogant jerks when you try to get them to do their jobs.

When you work for the government, doing your job is entirely optional.

Even when the Obama elites admit the government's failings, they still can't resist taking money and power from us and handing it over to the bureaucrats. Remember when President Obama announced the near-trillion-dollar stimulus plan? How he assured the American people that this time we could trust them?

> Here in Washington, we've all seen how quickly good intentions can turn into broken promises and wasteful spending. And with a plan of this scale [the stimulus] comes enormous responsibility to get it right.
>
> That is why I have asked Vice President Biden to lead a tough, unprecedented oversight effort—because nobody messes with Joe.

> I have told each member of my Cabinet as well as may-
> ors and governors across the country that they will be held
> accountable by me and the American people for every dol-
> lar they spend. I have appointed a proven and aggressive
> Inspector General to ferret out any and all cases of waste
> and fraud. And we have created a new website called recov-
> ery.gov so that every American can find out how and where
> their money is being spent.

So what happened? We spent more than 18 million in tax dollars
on a website—something you and I can do for $9.99 a month—
only to be told the "jobs created or saved" statistics posted there
were unreliable. Billions of stimulus dollars disappeared into the
black hole of bureaucracy. Government workers who got raises
were counted as "new hires" or "saved jobs." Congressional districts that didn't exist were flooded with magic tax dollars to create imaginary jobs.

Here's a more disturbing example: remember the Islamist
Crotch-Bomber of Christmas 2009? A Nigerian jihadist whose
name was in a U.S. terror database, whose own father had
reported him to U.S. authorities. But he was still able to keep his
U.S. visa, get on a plane in Amsterdam, and fly to Detroit. It
was in the skies over the Motor City that he tried to detonate the
PETN explosives sewn into his undies. His first attempt failed
because he screwed up the detonation. He didn't get a second
attempt because his fellow passengers jumped him and prevented it.

We then discover that this Islamist had been in touch with the
same al Qaeda-linked imam who'd inspired the Fort Hood
shooter a few months earlier. And still the Nigerian Naughty-Bits
Bomber had been able to board a U.S.-bound plane.

So what was the reaction from America's head of Homeland Security, Janet "Potential Domestic Terrorist" Napolitano? Dismal failure? Security disaster? Heads must roll?

Wrong. "Everything went according to clockwork," she told *ABC News* two days later. There was "no suggestion that [the bomber] was improperly screened," she stated on CNN. Other than that whole "bomb strapped to his Underoos" part, I assume. Nope. From her perspective as a lifelong government worker, Napolitano declared that "the system worked."

And, from her perspective, I guess it did. She got to keep her job.

Government: Making Strip Club Managers Look Good

This brings us back once again to the government porn business. When a talk-show guy like me gets a call from a stripper complaining about guys surfing porn, you know you've got a problem.

In this case, the stripper was Victoria—former stripper, actually—who spent ten years dancing at New England's finest "gentlemen's clubs." Miffed after hearing the story about rampant on-the-clock porn surfing at the National Science Foundation, she called my show to complain. Surfing porn on government time is such a waste that even strippers can't get away with it.

One day at work, Victoria asked a club manager if she could log onto the Internet to check her personal email. He told her the club ownership had taken away their Internet connection entirely. Why?

"They said the club managers were spending too much time looking at porn," she was told. "They're supposed to be in the club working, not looking at naked women."

Well, you get the point.

My point is that I'll be ready to support ObamaCare the day the average government bureaucrat works as smart and as hard as the employees at the Pink Pussycat Lounge.

And for you government workers reading this book on the job, no, they don't have a website.

Chapter Twelve

Don't Spread My Wealth, Spread My Work Ethic!

O f all the arguments made by American liberals that drive the rest of us crazy, nothing is more likely to induce hair-pulling anger from average Americans than extolling illegal immigrants for "doing jobs Americans won't do."

I can't speak for the San Fran swells or Ivy League grads who have this attitude, but on behalf of at least three generations of the Graham family, I can say with absolute certainty: there's no such thing as a job we won't do.

Mowing lawns, digging ditches, scrubbing pots and pans, cropping tobacco, waiting tables on the overnight shift at an L.A. greasy spoon—you can meet an American who's done every one of those jobs just by coming to my folks' house for dinner. And there are millions of homes like ours across this country.

My mom, the "Brooks Brother tea party hatermonger" with "no compassion for working people," for example, waited tables with *her* mom at a little coffee joint called Jody's in Torrance, California. My grandmother, Jane Futrell, grew up in abject poverty in Tulsa, Oklahoma, living for a time in a renovated boxcar that was part of a New Deal project. (Her brush with celebrity: she met Eleanor Roosevelt when the First Lady was touring the local community center.)

The only job these two Americans wouldn't do were the jobs they couldn't *find*.

Even now, I can't imagine my mother ever not working, even though she's reached the age of [redacted under threat that my mom will post my prom pictures on the Internet]. My mom will always be doing something worthwhile, productive, and labor-intensive because that's a vital element of her self-worth.

She works partly because she wants to, and partly because she's supposed to. And that's what most Americans do. We work. It's who we are. So why does our government work so hard to make work...so hard?

In an article entitled, "Why Work Doesn't Pay," *Forbes* magazine told the story of Judith Lederman, a Westchester County, New York, woman who was knocked out of her high-stress, high-responsibility, $120,000-a-year job by the economic crash. As months passed and Team Obama's economic policies took effect, she started looking at part-time, low-stress jobs that paid half as much—not because that was the best she could find, but because, in the era of Obama, working harder just doesn't pay.

Now, for the vast majority of Americans, $120,000 a year is good money. My mom would be happy to take that right now, thank you very much. So how can it make sense to turn it down for half the income?

"While the first $60,000 of her income would be lightly taxed, the next $60,000 would be hit with what is in effect a 79% tax rate," *Forbes* reported. As a result, all the work Ms. Lederman would do to earn that additional sixty grand would only net her a whopping $12,600.

But wait—who pays *79 percent* tax rates? Maybe some Richie-Rich like Warren Buffet, but not someone pulling down $120,000. That can't be right, can it?

Ah, there's the rub. It's not just that her actual tax rates went up with her increased income; it's also that her government benefits went down. By working harder and earning more, this 50-year-old mom would miss out on the taxpayer-funded goodies the government gives people who, well, don't work hard and earn more.

> How did a middle-class single mom wind up with a 79% marginal tax rate? At $120,000 she would pay $16,500 a year more in federal and state taxes, wouldn't qualify for the five-year $12,000-a-year cut in her mortgage payments she's applying for and would be eligible for $19,000 a year less in need-based college financial aid.

This is just one case, one woman, and one income bracket. But did you check that math? By *not* working as hard and *not* earning as much, she picks up a solid $31,000+ in cold, hard cash. And where does that dough come from?

The sucker who's workin' for a living—and who earns *less than the woman in this story!* In other words, from my mom.

Look, we all know the O-bots are going to "spread the wealth around." That's not news. Even that "greedy capitalist" George

W. Bush did the same thing. Under President Bush, government spending shot up 70 percent, according to the Cato Institute—and that doesn't include the deluge of TARP/bailout money during the banking crisis at the end of his term.

Who got most of that money? Yes, defense and security got a fair portion. But as the Heritage Foundation notes, President Bush "created a Medicare drug entitlement that will cost an estimated $800 billion in its first decade... [and] increased education spending 58 percent faster than inflation."

The historic explosion of spending and debt under President Obama obscures the fact that for years, the trend has been toward more government spending more money and doing more stuff. And if the liberal media would have listened to talk radio, they would have known that Americans were complaining about this spending long before the Obama administration.

Only after Scott Brown's historic upset in the Massachusetts Senate race did the public's rejection of debt and spending start to penetrate Washington. And even then, President Obama couldn't get serious. In his 2010 State of the Union speech, the president proposed a partial freeze on some portions of domestic spending. How partial? It only covered about 17 percent of the federal budget, totaling $250 billion over ten years. To put that in perspective, Obama's budget for the 2011 fiscal year alone is nearly $4 trillion. Over ten years, it's close to $40 trillion. So $250 billion isn't a spending "freeze." It's not even a spending "chill." It's an ice cube dropped into the spending furnace, a rounding error in the massive deluge of debt pouring out of Washington.

Taxpayers and tea partiers complained about the debt under Bush, and the reason they're complaining more now is because there's so much more debt. And why wouldn't we complain?

After all, regardless of who spent it, the same people have to pay for it: America's earners and achievers.

In 2000, the top 1 percent of American income earners paid 37 percent of the federal income tax burden. Under George W. "Tax Cuts for the Wealthy" Bush, that number actually rose to 40 percent, while about 10 million lower-income Americans fell from the tax rolls completely. Thanks to Bush, they ended up owing no income tax.

In fact, everyone at the 50 percent income mark or lower—half of American earners—paid a combined 3 percent of the federal income tax burden. That includes 43 million Americans who filed tax returns but paid *zero* federal income tax. None.

I think I speak for every tea partier in America when I say we'd all like to pay zero income taxes. We'd love it if tax money fell from the clouds above like manna, then was gathered by leprechauns and fed to magic unicorns that then provided government healthcare by curing us with a touch of their horn.

Unfortunately this plan—commonly known as "Obama's economic policy"—isn't going to work. Grown-ups understand this. The phrase "half of all Americans pay virtually no income tax" is great, until you add, "but the federal government is still adding trillions in new spending, and the other half of American workers have to pay it all!"

There's no way around it. The tea party movement is based on the acknowledgement that there's no such thing as a free lunch... and Chef Obama just added lobster and caviar to next year's menu.

Work Is for Losers

Typical Americans understand that if you work and your neighbor can't, the government is going to take some of your money and give it to your neighbor. Fine. But we also understand that if you work and your neighbor *won't*—the government does pretty much the same thing.

And now the push for ever more government involvement in our lives has shoved that income threshold higher under the Democratic Congress and, especially, under President Obama. And you can see that in the case of the Westchester mother above. Is $60,000 poor? Not in most of the U.S., where the average household income is around $47,000. Can this woman work more and earn more? Absolutely.

But *should* she? My mom would say, "If you want the money, yes." But the O-bots say, "Not so fast. We might be able to shake down your neighbors so you can spend more time at home watching Judge Judy and still have the same lifestyle. It's the new American way!"

Ask Cheryl Morse, a tax practitioner in Massachusetts who told *Forbes*,

> Don't think the American public is stupid. People call me and say, "What's the most I can earn before I lose the earned income tax credit?" [They] may not understand marginal rates, but they're shocked when they lose the college or child credits. You hear all the time, "The harder I work, the more they take away from me."

And it's even worse for Americans foolish enough to start their own small businesses. Liberals in Congress, for example, keep pushing for surtaxes on the "rich" to pay for healthcare and other government programs. But as the *Wall Street Journal* reports, a tax on individuals earning more than $280,000 a year would pound small business owners and investors, who make up more than 60 percent of those filers. In fact, almost half of all the income this surtax would raise would come from sole proprietorships and subchapter S corporations—in other words, small business owners, not corporate bigwigs.

You don't work? Don't worry—the government will make your neighbors give you healthcare and housing. You do work? All bets are off. You'll lose benefits and pick up higher taxes. You start your own business and hire other people to work for you? You're doomed.

"I almost understand why some people stay on welfare," a self-employed house cleaner told *Forbes*. She wanted a new, lower interest rate on her condo, but by working harder and earning more money, she could lose that opportunity. You work, you lose.

Jobs Americans Can't Find

Of course, all this is academic to Americans who can't find a job. And it's no coincidence that the rise of the tea party movement paralleled the rise in unemployment.

I don't think the Left has truly grasped the impact 10 percent unemployment has on typical Americans. In Europe (a.k.a. "Barack Obama's America"), double-digit joblessness is no big deal. Happens all the time.

But not in the United States. Americans define ourselves by our work. Liberals give lip service to the idea, but when the economic crisis hit, what was their priority?

- spending nearly a trillion dollars "stimulating" new government
- trying to adopt an anti-business, anti-free-market healthcare "reform"

- attempting to force through a "cap and trade" global warming bill

Here's the problem: none of this had anything to do with creating jobs. Months of lobbying and arm twisting and debate and name-calling and cries that the very fate of our republic was at stake—for what? Government programs that, at best, would create no jobs and, more likely, would actually kill them.

When the O-bots pushed through the stimulus, for example, Obama's chief economic advisor, Christina Romer, assured us that unemployment would top out at 8 percent. Her testimony featured a now-infamous chart projecting unemployment with and without a stimulus. What happened? Unemployment went higher *with* the stimulus (10.2 percent) than the Obama administration

Love Letter from the Left

"Absolutely amazing poll results from CNN today about the $787 [billion] stimulus package: nearly three out of four Americans think the money has been wasted. On second thought, they may be right: it's been wasted *on them*.... This is yet further evidence that Americans are flagrantly ill-informed and, for those watching Fox News, misinformed.... It is very difficult to thrive in an increasingly competitive world if you're a nation of dodos."

—*Time* magazine writer Joe Klein, bemoaning the American people's inability to understand how successful the stimulus was, in a blog post titled, "Too Dumb to Thrive" projected it would go if we'd done nothing. We were out nearly a trillion bucks, and an additional 2.5 million Americans were out of a job in the ten months after the stimulus passed.

To typical Americans, this is a disaster. We're blowing hundreds of billions and still losing jobs? Sound the alarm! Set a new course! Dive! Dive! Dive!

In the White House? You didn't hear a peep. No change, just more of the same. There was no political battle over jobs. All the arguing was about healthcare and cap and trade. Meanwhile, Obama's idea of good economic news is when unemployment doesn't go up as fast as expected.

And millions of out-of-work Americans are watching this in utter astonishment. The folks back home are fighting to keep their homes and their jobs, and their representatives are in Washington fighting insurance companies, FOX News, and people who visit the "wrong" websites?

It's really no surprise that a movement protesting all this suddenly appeared. Watching the Washington death match over higher taxes and healthcare reform in the middle of a recession, the question isn't, "Who's crazy enough to go to a tea party?" but rather, "Who's crazy enough not to?"

No Americans Need Apply

All of this makes the disconnect over illegal immigration even more mindboggling. When the O-bots hear talk radio listeners complain that ObamaCare will give taxpayer-funded health insurance to criminal immigrants, they think the conversation is about race or ethnic identity. No matter how many times my Boston callers complain about our thousands of Irish illegals, for example, local liberals insist me and my listeners are all racists.

There are many sides to the illegal immigration debate, from issues of fundamental fairness (rewarding cheaters is wrong) to cultural unity and cohesion. But more than anything else, illegal immigration is a jobs issue.

When unemployment is below 5 percent, this debate is a more theoretical conversation about the principle that no one should be above the law: "What part of 'illegal' don't you understand?" But when the real unemployment rate for young, black Americans with just a high school education hits 39 percent as it did in 2009—and the rate for native-born Hispanics reaches 35 per-cent—the issue becomes much more pragmatic: "What part of, 'There's an American who needs a job to feed his family but can't because you're paying Eduardo under the table to landscape your yard' don't you understand?"

Liberal amnesty advocates tacitly concede that point when they invoke the "jobs Americans won't do" argument. Most Ameri-cans recognize there are jobs, and there are Americans who need them. But, Team Obama claims, the two can never meet—not even during a recession.

To typical Americans, this is insanity. And in December 2009, when congressional liberals followed the screw-u-lus package, the healthcare bill, and the cap-and-trade bill by introducing the "Comprehensive Immigration Reform for America's Security and Prosperity Act of 2009 (CIR ASAP)," job-seeking Americans began to ask if the Democratic Party had lost its collective mind.

Here it was, Christmastime 2009. Unemployment was still above 10 percent. Mom and Dad were poring over the newspa-per looking for work, and what did they find? Ads for Christmas presents they can't afford to give their own kids, and news stories about Congress trying to give the last few jobs away to illegal immigrants.

Merry Christmas!

And yes, that's what we white supremacist, teabagging, yahoo extremists call people who immigrate to America illegally—"illegal immigrants." We don't call them "undocumented workers" because at least 30 percent of illegal immigrants don't work. It would be like calling me an "unemployed gigolo." Flattering thought, but hardly accurate.

The euphemism "undocumented worker" conveys the absurd notion that these "workers" simply lack a few needless, bureaucratic documents. But there's nothing unusual or unfair about requiring documentation. Having the right paperwork is the difference between "registered pharmacist" and "drug dealer." And what is a bank robbery other than an "undocumented" cash withdrawal?

"Undocumented worker" is a meaningless phrase, like "rap music" or "redneck culture." An illegal alien's problem isn't that he doesn't have his documents handy, but rather that he never bothered to get them. And if you find the transformation of "illegal aliens" into "undocumented workers" baffling, try this real-life headline from the *Arizona Daily Star*: "Entrant-Rights Rally Falls Short Of Mark."

They're not "aliens," or even "immigrants." They're *entrants*. And it turns out they have rights—the right, apparently, to take construction jobs from legal immigrants and U.S. citizens, smack-dab in the middle of a recession.

The combination of stupidity, insult, and unfairness that defines the amnesty movement enrages me, but it doesn't come close to how naturalized citizens feel about it. These are the legal immi..., uh, make that the "migra...," that is, the "entrants" who came to America, stood in line, paid the fees, took the tests, and earned the legal right to work and raise their families here.

Today many of these legal immigrants are U.S. citizens. And not only are they forced to compete with criminal immigrants for jobs, but liberals also want to reward the criminals with the same standing as those who did the right thing.

Watching a work crew of immigrants building a public school in America should be a sight that makes us all proud. People from the rest of the world admire America so much, they're willing to jump through hoops for a chance to join us in building the greatest nation in the world.

But imagine how it looks to an unemployed American construction worker (true story). He worked for years, paid his taxes, and now that money is building that school—and paying criminal immigrants to do a job he could be doing. It's not inspiring. It's outrageous.

The same is true every time a working American sees his tax dollars go to rewarding criminal behavior. American liberals dismiss these concerns by shifting attention to the small stuff: how much money does it cost to give criminal immigrants the same college tuition subsidies as legal residents? A few million bucks? That's chickenfeed in a country that can afford a $787 billion stimulus.

But that's just an excuse to ignore the main point—that taking from legal citizens to pay for benefits to illegal immigrants is indefensible.

The Associated Press reported on a program at the University of California at San Diego where faculty used tax dollars to design special GPS-enabled cell phones to help criminal immigrants safely sneak across the border from Mexico.

"The effort is being done on the government's dime—an irony not lost on the designers whose salaries are paid by the state of California," reported the AP. "'There are many, many areas in which every American would say I don't like the way my tax dollars are being spent. Our answer to that is an in-your-face, so what?' says UCSD lecturer Brett Stalbaum."

Don't like paying to help people come steal your job? Tough luck! Sit down and shut up!

During the debate over ObamaCare and whether illegal immigrants should get subsidized healthcare, NPR's Juan Williams said, "I think it's in our national interest to make sure we don't have sick people on our streets."

And you know what—he's right! It's so unfair. After all, according to Michael Moore and Barack Obama (among others), we've got one of the worst medical systems in the world. These unwell citizens of Mexico, Ireland, Brazil, and Ukraine shouldn't be stuck here with our lousy healthcare system. Cuba's got us beat by a mile. That's why liberals were so desperate to destroy...um, "reform" the healthcare system. It's too expensive, too unjust, too unfair.

What kind of heartless, mean-spirited bastards would keep these poor, undocumented, and unwell "entrants" trapped in America's awful system? Not me. I say it's time to have a heart. Do the right thing. Let's deport these fine folks to their home countries, so they can escape our healthcare injustices and get the outstanding medical treatment one finds in Tijuana, Tipperary, Rio, and Odessa.

In fact, when I think of what a bigoted, hate-filled nation this is, with millions of deranged, gun-toting, teabagging rednecks, I fear for the estimated 12 million "pre-documented immigrants" living here. Democratic leaders insist we must move forward with amnesty and legalization, and once again I'm proud to say they're right. "Amnesty and legalization"—that's the talk radio/tea party solution! Here's how it would work.

First, the U.S. government agrees to grant amnesty to every criminal immigrant currently here. Given that it's against the law to enter our nation illegally—and impossible to remain here without committing tax fraud, identity fraud, and other felonies—such amnesty is no small matter. Not to mention all the unpaid taxes, the educational and medical services consumed, etc.

Well, we typical Americans are prepared to wipe that slate clean—total amnesty for all violations of civil and criminal law. That's a lot for us mean ol' American bigots—but we're trying.

Once true amnesty is granted and all the crimes committed by illegals to get here and stay here are forgiven, we are prepared to make them all legal citizens overnight. How? By returning them to the country where they have legal status. An Irishman working construction in Connecticut is an illegal immigrant. When he's doing it in Dublin, he's a righteous citizen!

Voila—problem solved! Nobody has to be prosecuted, everyone gets to be legal, and we still protect those quirky concepts oddly treasured by rightwing tea partiers, like "national sovereignty" and the "rule of law." Everybody wins.

How bizarre is it that this suggestion is dismissed as a joke, while rewarding illegals for stealing American jobs is viewed as completely rational? The idea that the government should side with legal immigrants and Americans is simply rejected out of hand. The notion that it should be harder to cheat and live illegally in the U.S. than it is to live and work here honestly is, for some reason, unacceptable.

The fact is, folks like my mom who work for a living, who play by the rules, and who expect the rules to apply to everyone just don't have any juice in Washington. Nobody is on their side. They used to be solid citizens, now they're nothing but chumps.

And the O-bots seem surprised that these chumps want to take their country back.

Chapter Thirteen

"It's the People's Seat": The Scott Brown Story

When the revolution came to Massachusetts in 2010, I had a front-row seat. And it was in Scott Brown's pick-up truck.

Senator Scott Brown was a regular caller to my Boston talk radio show long before he won the biggest political upset victory in U.S. history and became the "Scott Heard 'Round the World."

How did a fiscally conservative, tough-on-terror Republican win liberal Ted Kennedy's Senate seat in the bluest of blue states? How did a relatively unknown state senator beat a Democratic attorney general in a state where Democrats outnumber Republicans three to one? How did a guy who spent most of the campaign driving his pick-up across the state, meeting voters, and shaking hands beat the entire Massachusetts Democratic party, the liberal media, and even President Obama himself?

Months later, I still can't believe it. How *did* that happen? I was there, but I'm not absolutely sure. In fact, just ten days before the special election in January, I was telling my listeners it was all but impossible for Scott Brown to win that election.

And being the big-mouth that I am, I told Scott Brown the same thing. I urged him not to waste his time "trying to win," but instead to focus on forcing his opponent, Martha Coakley, to defend unpopular policies like ObamaCare and treating terrorists like civilian criminals. That way, I told him, he could begin swaying independents, who would hopefully help Republicans win the "realistic" races for governor and the state legislature later in the year.

But actually winning the election? Don't kid yourself. And I'm not ashamed to admit my defeatism; in fact, I still insist there's no way Scott Brown wins that race. And I've got the facts to prove it.

Look at the political environment Brown faced when he decided to run for the U.S. Senate. Of Massachusetts' twelve federal elected officials—two senators and ten congressmen—all twelve were Democrats. No Republican had even come close to winning one of those seats in more than a decade. The last time Massachusetts had a Republican senator, Richard Nixon wasn't just president—he was still popular. The last time a non-incumbent Republican won a Senate race was 1966.

In 2009, Republicans weren't doing much better at the state level. Every constitutional office from governor to auditor was held by a Democrat. In the forty-member Massachusetts state senate, there were a whopping five Republicans. It gives new meaning to the old joke that "the entire [fill-in-the-blank] Republican Party could hold a meeting in a booth at Denny's." Except in Massachusetts, they can't even fill a six-top.

Meanwhile, Democrats controlled 90 percent of the seats in the Massachusetts House of Representatives. And the re-election rate for incumbents was even higher. Every big city in the state—Boston, Worcester, Springfield—had Democratic mayors with political machines that could crank out votes. The state Democratic Party was large and well-funded, too. The Massachusetts state GOP, in contrast, was smaller than a typical PTO bake sale committee.

Here's how bad it looked for Scott Brown: in a Suffolk University poll in September 2009, Martha Coakley beat him by 30 points—a margin so big it usually doesn't exist in politics. It was no surprise, then, that when Coakley ran in a four-way Democratic primary, more people voted *for the guy who came in second*—Congressman Michael Capuano—than voted in the entire GOP primary that day.

In short, Scott Brown didn't have a chance. And still, he won. Why?

There were several reasons: the candidate, the opposition, the moment—but the most important of all was the people.

Meet Scott Brown

Before we get to the everyday voters who made history in Massachusetts, let's take a look at the guy they elected. To Republicans across the country, Scott Brown is now a political superstar. But here in Massachusetts, I know him better as "Scott from Wrentham," a regular talk radio listener and caller. In a state with so few Republicans, every elected member of the party stands out to a degree, but I have to say that State Senator Brown wasn't viewed as particularly exceptional.

It's true he got into the state senate in 2004 by winning a tough special election whose timing was manipulated by the legislature to benefit the Democrat. (One Massachusetts insider reportedly said, "We cheated and he still beat us!") But inside the state house, he was considered just another guy.

A Lieutenant Colonel with thirty years' service in the National Guard, Scott often appeared on my radio station to discuss military issues. And he was a dependable voice for fiscal conservatism, which is the brand of Republicanism most popular in Massachusetts.

Okay, he'd posed nude for *Cosmopolitan* magazine years ago to help pay for law school, but that sure didn't bring him fame or fortune. In fact, he was probably best known for the women in his life. His wife, Gail Huff, is a popular Boston news personality, and his daughter Ayla is a Boston College basketball star and an *American Idol* alum with a CD and hit single.

But Scott Brown, it turned out, had two powerful political assets. The first was his work ethic. When few people gave him any chance to win his senate race, he spent day after day crisscrossing Massachusetts to meet with voters at diners, train stations, picnics, and parades.

The second asset was his willingness to listen. Scott Brown had firm political principles, but he didn't start his senate campaign with an agenda. Instead, he listened to voters. Early on, he picked up on their frustration, the rising anger with the arrogance and indifference of their public "servants."

After the election, I was flattered when Senator-elect Brown credited my radio show with helping him win. But it didn't surprise me that he liked talk radio, because he was genuinely interested in the concerns of everyday people. While the political class was content to read its own talking points in the *Boston Globe-Democrat*, Scott was listening to "Dave in Chelsea," "Sue in Amherst," and "Jonathan in Dorchester."

There's something in the media/theater biz known as "getting it in your ear." It means you understand your subject or audience so well that when you speak, they hear themselves. Scott Brown had the talk radio audience "in his ear." Anyone who could read polls in 2009 knew support for ObamaCare was tanking, but Scott could tell you *why* people didn't like it, what parts of the plan bothered them. And when he spoke, the voters could hear that he had listened.

He understood the issues like a politician, but he approached them like a regular guy. And this made him the polar opposite of his opponent.

Meet Martha Coakley

Scott Brown's greatest strength may have been his excellent taste in opponents. Simon Cowell could have held nationwide auditions and not found a better opposing candidate than Massachusetts attorney general Martha Coakley.

In the end, Coakley's Senate campaign wasn't the Hindenburg. It wasn't the Titanic. It was the Hindenburg *crashing into* the Titanic.

If Republicans thought Brown would probably lose, Democrats *knew* it. Dems in general, and Coakley in particular, assumed voters would dutifully "vote the 'D'" regardless of who the candidate was. Summing up the feelings of the liberal establishment, *Boston Globe* columnist Charles Pierce published an open letter to Scott Brown assessing his prospects:

> [Y]ou have approximately the same chance of filling [the Senate seat] as you did the pilot's chair of the Starship Enterprise.... [T]he notion that Massachusetts would elect a Republican to fill the seat left vacant by Edward Kennedy was the property of people who buy interesting mushrooms in interesting places. You might as well expect the House of

Windsor to be succeeded on the British throne by the Kardashian sisters.

Having served one term as attorney general, Coakley wasn't exactly a household name, but in political circles she was well-known for her oversized political ambitions. In 2004, when she was just a country district attorney, she was already eyeing John Kerry's senate seat in case he won the presidency. And she provoked criticism with her decision to start campaigning for the Senate seat formerly occupied by Ted Kennedy before his funeral had even been held. Warm and fuzzy she is not.

In the four-way Democratic primary, Martha Coakley campaigned largely on identity politics: Massachusetts had never elected a female senator or governor, and she was the one to change that. She also campaigned on terrorism; in a Massachusetts Democratic primary, that meant she stridently opposed the death penalty for terrorists.

Although she easily won the primary, there were early signs she would be a catastrophic candidate. During one of the few debates she agreed to participate in, Coakley argued she was qualified to handle foreign policy because "I have a sister who lives overseas, and she's been in England and now lives in the Middle East." It was a lot like Sarah Palin's "I can see Russia from my house" line—except that Palin didn't actually say anything that dumb. Coakley did.

Coakley didn't disguise her expectation that the race against Scott Brown was just a formality ending in her coronation. It's hard to find another message in her decision to go on vacation just six weeks before Election Day. Her regal attitude provided the perfect contrast for Scott Brown's populist message that "it's not Ted Kennedy's seat. It's the people's seat."

When she did lower herself to campaigning, Martha met with politicians, not typical people. Asked about this inside-politics strategy, she mocked the idea of pressing flesh with the common folk. "What should I be doing—standing outside Fenway Park in the cold, shaking hands?"

What? Put on a jacket and go meet the peasants? And at a baseball park, too? Why, I bet they don't even serve Grey Poupon!

Coakley was just terrible. She tried to avoid televised debates, and she demonstrated a fundamental lack of understanding of the key issues, including ObamaCare, which she strongly supported nonetheless. She was also uninformed on terrorism, insisting there were no terrorists or Taliban members in Afghanistan. This was news to the American families who lost servicemembers to terror attacks in Afghanistan just hours before Coakley made this idiotic claim.

"That was when I knew I was going to win this race," Scott Brown told me the night of his victory. "She knew she had made a mistake, I could see it in her eyes. Then when I got off stage and found out she had started running negative attack ads that night, I told myself, 'I'm going to win this thing.'" In contrast to Coakley, Brown proposed a clear anti-terror strategy: "In dealing with terrorists, our tax dollars should pay for weapons to stop them, not lawyers to defend them." He wanted to treat terrorists like enemy combatants, lock them up at Guantanamo Bay, and use all legal means to interrogate them about other terrorist plots.

Coakley's campaign largely comprised a never-ending series of gaffes. In a state where the Red Sox-Yankee rivalry carries a near-religious significance, Coakely claimed Red Sox legend Curt Schilling was a Yankee fan. In an overwhelmingly Catholic state, she told pro-life Catholics they "probably shouldn't work" in emergency rooms in case a rape victim needed abortion services.

228

As Brown surged she resorted to increasingly strident attack ads, but these were problematic as well; she pulled one ad because it misspelled the name of her own state, then she pulled another because it sparked an outcry by superimposing a photo of Scott Brown over a pre-9/11 picture of the World Trade Center.

How bad was Coakley's campaign? Just days after an earthquake killed some 200,000 people in Haiti and left millions homeless and hungry, UN Envoy to Haiti Bill Clinton came to Boston for a Coakley fundraiser. Haiti was in ruins, but Clinton apparently decided Coakley's campaign was an even bigger disaster.

Then came the infamous Coakley Cramdown.

The day after the final debate, with polls showing she was now in a real race, Coakley jetted off to D.C. for a fundraiser. And not just any fundraiser. It was hosted almost entirely by Washington lobbyists with ties to Big Pharma and other healthcare business interests, thus highlighting Coakley's support for the unpopular inside-the-Beltway ObamaCare plan.

That was bad enough. But Coakley found a way to make it worse.

Leaving the big-wig reception, she stopped for a few press questions. But she studiously ignored the *Weekly Standard*'s John McCormack when he asked if she stood by her statement that there are no terrorists in Afghanistan. As she walked away, McCormack tried to follow her with the rest of the press gaggle. A Coakley campaign aide then shoved him into a fence and knocked him down. After helping him up, the aide shoved him several more times, physically blocking him from getting near Coakley, who looked on impassively and then turned and walked away.

The incident was emblematic of politics today. What did John McCormack do? He asked a politician a tough question.

Martha Coakley should have answered the guy. Instead, he was ignored and then assaulted for daring to challenge the political class.

As I watched the video, I thought of my talk radio listeners. Of the people I'd met at tea party rallies. Of folks like my mom.

What have they done? They asked some questions. They spoke out against higher spending, rising debt, fat bailouts, and other unpopular polices that Washington liberals keep shoving down our throats.

These regular people showed up at a tea party or a townhall meeting just to be heard. They wanted their public servants to respond to concerns of the public. And what happened? They were insulted, dismissed, shoved aside.

Like that reporter, these votes have been pushed to the curb. Forget getting an answer—how dare you even *ask*? Watching Coakley's goon work over McCormack, I wondered how many other voters saw that guy spread out on the ground at the hands of some political flak and thought to themselves, "Pal, I know just how you feel."

After film of that incident got out, the race was over. Coakley had pushed, but the good people of Massachusetts pushed back even harder. They took a senate seat that had been held by a Kennedy of Hyannisport since 1953 and gave it to a pick-up driving Republican from Wrentham.

And Last But Not Least...

As great a candidate as Scott Brown turned out to be, and as incompetent as Coakley was, Brown's victory would have been impossible without the enormous efforts of one man:

President Barack Obama.

I can't speak for the rest of America, but President Obama has brought true "hope and change" to New England conservatives and Republicans. In 2008, the local GOP nearly disappeared. There were no candidates in the wings and no hope on the horizon. Then came the era of Obama. In November 2008, Obama got 62 percent of the Massachusetts vote—one of his biggest margins of victory in the nation.

In January 2010, a Zogby poll showed Obama neck-and-neck for the presidency in a theoretical match-up with . . . Scott Brown. Silly, I know. After all, Scott was only a first-term senator who had just come from the state senate and had no executive experience. America would never send someone so inexperienced to the White Hou . . .

Never mind.

Scott Brown won deep-blue Massachusetts by running against the policies of President Obama. Not against the man himself, but against his politics. In fact, Brown's campaign didn't have an angry word for Coakley at all. He was repeatedly trashed by the Coakley campaign and other Democrats with vile, lie-filled ads. ("1,736 women were raped in Massachusetts in 2008. Scott Brown wants hospitals to turn them all away.") But Scott kept smiling.

Meanwhile, he pointedly attacked the arrogance of Obama's Washington allies, the shamelessness of the backroom deals that were cut to pass ObamaCare, and the weakness of the administration's terrorism policies.

It worked. Massachusetts voters rejected Obama policies as too liberal even for them. People who had never voted Republican in their lives stood in line to work for Scott Brown so they could send a message to Washington.

That's the wave Scott Brown rode to the Senate. Yes, there was a local tide for change thanks to the hamfisted leadership of the corrupt Democratic machine in Massachusetts, and the haughty, inept Democratic governor Deval Patrick. But Barack Obama was the force behind the gale winds that pushed Scott Brown over the top.

Tea partiers played a key role in the grassroots effort behind the Brown campaign. Brown himself was not a tea party activist, and some of his positions were to the left of the tea party crowd. But I

> ## Love Letter from the Left
>
> "In Scott Brown we have an irresponsible, homophobic, racist, reactionary, ex-nude model, teabagging supporter of violence against women and against politicians with whom he disagrees."
>
> —Keith Olbermann

saw the same people at his campaign headquarters as I saw at our Boston Harbor tea party in April.

The tea partiers' support for Brown surprised some leftwing talking heads who believed their own rhetoric about tea partiers being ideological zealots somewhere to the right of Attila the Hun. But it all made perfect sense. Attracted by Brown's commonsense politics and his instinctive distrust of Washington's ability to solve problems, tea party networks combined with networks of the state's talk radio listeners to form the most energized, enthusiastic grassroots base I've seen in all my years watching or working on political campaigns.

This was evident in Brown's fundraising. GOP online strategist Patrick Ruffini, who handled the online donation technology for the Brown campaign, reported that in the final two weeks of the race, Brown raised more than $12 million online from more than 157,000 individual donations. On a single day, the Friday before the election, the campaign raised $2.2 million from more than 25,000 people.

But the people of Massachusetts wanted to do more than just give money. In a typical campaign, the hardest part is getting people actually to do things like show up at events and make phone calls. They all talk a good game, but what you usually end up with is a small group of hardcore activists begging folks just to put a sign in their yards. That's why money is so important—so campaigns can pay people to do the work.

Scott Brown had the opposite problem. In the last three weeks of the campaign, people were jamming themselves into his campaign offices demanding something to do. Instead of begging people to make phone calls, the Brown campaign had volunteers waiting in line for access to a telephone.

And perhaps the most amazing example of this passion was found in the homemade signs.

"Homemade signs?" I can't tell you how astonishing that concept is in today's politics. The Brown campaign printed thousands of signs, ran out, printed more, ran out again . . . and still couldn't keep up with the demand.

So Scott's determined supporters made their own. Some were magic marker on poster board, others were hand painted and carefully designed. I even saw trucks, covered in winter salt and sand, that had hand-drawn signs in their dirty cab windows. Anything to get out the simple message that they passionately wanted to be heard by Washington.

And heard they were. Massachusetts voters—not Mississippi or Montana, but *Massachusetts*—stopped ObamaCare in its tracks. And they affected other Obama policies as well. It was no coincidence that shortly after the election, the administration began backing away from its plan to try September 11 mastermind Khalid

Sheikh Mohammed in New York City. Additionally, two weeks after Brown's win, President Obama's State of the Union address featured uncharacteristic calls for a spending freeze and more off-shore oil drilling. That's like Fidel Castro announcing he was joining the Libertarian Party.

In 2008, America elected President Obama based on a nebulous hope for some undefined "change." In 2010, the voters of Massachusetts brought America real change with the election of a single senator.

"I Am Scott Brown!"

And suddenly, *everyone* was Scott Brown.

On the Sunday before the election, President Obama came to Massachusetts and mocked Scott Brown and his pick-up truck. "Don't get in that truck," Obama warned, "you might not like where it takes you." But two days after Brown's upset victory, Obama claimed, "The same thing that swept Scott Brown into office swept me into office." Likewise, liberal Massachusetts governor Deval Patrick, a strong backer of Martha Coakley, suddenly discovered that he "had a lot in common with Scott Brown."

Then came this jaw-dropping exchange between Chris Wallace and White House spokesflak Robert Gibbs on *Fox News Sunday*:

> **Wallace:** But, Robert, Scott Brown had a clear platform, and let's lay it out—stop health care, cut taxes, end backroom deals with special interest, and don't give terrorists Miranda rights.
>
> It wasn't the same thing that swept Barack Obama into office. Scott Brown explicitly campaigned against the Obama agenda.

> **Gibbs**: Well, that may be what he campaigned on, but that's not why the voters of Massachusetts sent him to Washington.

That's what he campaigned on, but it's not why people voted for him? That line will, I predict, end up in the Stupid Political Quotes Hall of Fame.

After Brown's win, the airwaves were filled with spinmeisters making the mind-bending argument that the reason Massachusetts defeated a Democrat endorsed by Obama was because they supported Obama. And the voters were so mad about the eight years of George W. Bush, they decided to punish him by electing a Republican to replace Ted Kennedy. President Obama himself learned from the election that "people are angry, not just because of what happened the last year or two years, but the last eight years."

That mean ol' Bush, we'll show him. We'll start electing *Republicans*! And if we're really, really mad—we'll elect a Republican president in 2012. How 'bout *them* apples, Mr. Bush?

Yes, it's idiotic, I know. But as they say, "How do you explain to someone who just doesn't get it, that the problem is they just don't get it?" There's a point where blind arrogance becomes comic, and we passed the punch line long ago. Two days after Scott Brown's victory, the *Boston Globe-Democrat* ran an op-ed by its former editorial-page editor with this headline: "The Message: Loud But Not So Clear."

Not clear to whom? Bad policies and even worse politics drove blue-state Massachusetts to replace Ted Kennedy with a fiscally conservative Republican. It wasn't exactly a subtle message.

And yet it's still lost on liberals who, when not hailing the election as a victory for Obamanomics, blamed the outcome on the poor quality of the voters. "Brown didn't run a hate campaign," the *Globe-Democrat*'s Renee Loth grudgingly conceded, "but he did become the locus for a broad variety of resentments, from people angry over the state's sales tax increase to changes in their healthcare to gay rights."

"Gay rights?" Were there any Brown ads about gay rights? Doesn't matter. Liberals can read between the lines: "Brown's campaign unmistakably appealed to men, even beyond the obvious contrast with Coakley," Loth continued. "The truck, the barn jacket, the sports figures giving endorsements all signaled that Brown's campaign was a comfortable home for disaffected men. Even his victory party...had the look and feel of a beer-fueled tailgate party."

Who knew that the key electorate in liberal Massachusetts was beer-swilling, truck-loving, testosterone-addled, homophobic white men? This from a state that elected a black governor, Deval Patrick, and just a year earlier gave Barack Obama a 26-point win!

Wow—what are they putting in that beer, anyway?

Once again, don't worry. This "logic" may be laughable to you, but it makes perfect sense to the liberal elites.

"Mobs Rule" was the predictable headline for *New York Times* columnist Charles Blow. "Welcome to the mob: an angry, wounded electorate, riled by recession, careening across the political spectrum, still craving change, nursing a bloodlust." These ignorant voters who are "too easily manipulated" acted in irrational anger, Blow insisted. It had nothing whatsoever to do with the fact that Team Obama's first year in office has been a stumbling, inept, and expensive mess. The common folk can't possibly be rejecting failed liberal policies. Why, all the little people love the Left. Just ask John Kerry.

This was the battle line between Scott Brown and the Obama establishment: the governing elites vs. We, the People. This is the struggle that continues today, and will go on as long as the Obama elites insist that what America needs is not better policies, but better citizens.

And again I think of those signs. Cardboard, hand-written, slapped-together, self-organized signs. These weren't the campaign tools of a political party or organized machine. These were the protest signs of typical Americans who saw a spark of real hope—a chance to stop the madness of the loony Left, to answer the arrogance of the Washington elite. They saw the opportunity and they rushed to seize it. That's why they rushed to Scott Brown, their smiling, optimistic advocate of change.

This was the same spirit I've seen at tea party after tea party. It's the same determination to confront abusive political power that you see at townhalls. It's the answer to that question I get so often from callers: "Yes, Michael—but what can we *do*?"

What these typical Americans in Massachusetts did was to win an unwinnable race, create the biggest political upset in U.S. history, and change the course of an entire nation.

And it all started in the back of one guy's pick-up truck.

The Party of "For"

"The tea party movement is a large, fractious confederation of Americans who are defined by what they are against. They are against the concentrated power of the educated class.... Personally, I'm not a fan of this movement."

—David Brooks, the *New York Times*, January 4, 2010

Wrong again.

David Brooks, a writer I often admire, speaks for the media and establishment elites when he condemns the supposed negativity of talk radio listeners, tea partiers, and typical Americans. We heard this same caricature when big-government liberals were defeated in Virginia, New Jersey, and especially in Massachusetts in 2009 and 2010.

At the time, pundits dismissed the voters as an "angry mob" too dumb to vote their own best interests. Finding refuge in self-delusion, the White House even argued that the election in ultra-liberal Massachusetts of Republican Scott Brown, who promised to provide the final vote to kill ObamaCare in the Senate, was actually an expression of anger at Obama's *opponents*.

Writing after Brown's victory, columnist Charles Krauthammer captured the condescension underlying the Democrats' image of the impulsive, angry voter: "That implies an inchoate, unthinking lashing-out at whoever happens to be in power—even at your liberal betters who are forcing on you an agenda that you can't even see is in your own interest."

Krauthammer is right. This wasn't unthinking anger or a partisan rejection of Democratic policies. These "typical" Americans—and I'm proud to count myself among them—believe in something, something so powerful, so profound, so central to who we are as a people, that we're willing to walk the gauntlet of catcalls, taunts, and attacks to stand and defend it.

We believe in liberty. We believe in freedom. We believe in opportunity, responsibility, and accountability. In fact, we don't just believe in them.

We *live* them.

Why do we drag ourselves out of bed in the morning and schlep our way to work every day—knowing that at least half (if not more) of what we earn will be snatched from us and our families by tax collectors from Washington to the local Wal-mart check out? Why?

Because we believe in individual responsibility. We want an America where people work and take responsibility for themselves and their families, rather than waiting for the government to come bail them out. So we live our values by getting our assets off the couch and going to work.

Why do so many American families, including many poor families, find a way for the moms to stay home when their children are young and need them most? Because we believe in the future, and in our responsibility to create the best possible future for our kids. And we believe in our duty to create the best generation of citizens we can.

But why don't these moms rail against a government that doesn't "give" them "free" money to stay home? Why don't they demand child care on someone else's dime? Because they're living their values of personal accountability. If someone offered them a free ride, they wouldn't take it. They don't want one.

Why do busy taxpayers, many of them struggling every day to pay their bills and raise their families, make time to attend a rally at some public park or government plaza on a work day, just for the privilege of standing in the sun for hours and being denounced by the media?

All that effort, just to complain about the debt our government is placing on our children, the assault on our principles of liberty and self-reliance, the policies that promote government dependence and irresponsible spending—it's all so abstract. There's no immediate pay-off for them, no dollop of government cash to be gained. Why do they go to so much trouble? Why do they bother to show up at all?

It's not just because they're "against" Obama or the "educated class" or clueless leftwing nuts or anyone else. They could stay home and complain about Washington by calling my talk show.

But they do show up. They do march. And they're marching not *against*, but *for*.

Why We Fight

What are we for? First and foremost, we are for freedom. And I don't mean we paid attention in civics class or that we can quote Patrick Henry from memory. Freedom is more than that, and it's also more than the mere absence of tyranny. We are for freedom as a force for good, in and of itself.

Granted, all politicians declare their support for freedom, along with mom, apple pie, and pork barrel spending. But that's just Hallmark card boilerplate. The people who call my radio show and go to tea parties truly believe in the power of liberty.

We're not showing up at townhall meetings just to oppose liberal policies and to mock the Left's heavy-handed, big-government ineptitude. We're there fighting for freedom, because we believe free men are better men, and that free people, free minds, and free markets make the best, most prosperous America.

We believe in opportunity. But that isn't a government-based guarantee of success—opportunity is the chance to fail, too. While Brooks's "educated class" is trying to take away the possibility of failure, while it's declaring its favorite Wall Street businesses "too big to fail," we're defending the very premise of the land of opportunity.

That's why we're also fighting for responsibility. Every bailout, every government rescue of some citizen from his own bad behavior, is a blow against our values. We don't treasure these values because we read them in a book, or because they sound nice. We know the future of our entire nation is at stake if our fellow citizens abandon these virtues for the easy vices of government dependency.

Achievement, opportunity, and accountability must be celebrated together, otherwise none of them truly exist.

And most of all, we're for democracy and the consent of the governed. This principle—that this land is our land—is perhaps Americans' most precious civic ideal. And it should be one of the most basic. After all, it seems self-evident (right, Mr. Jefferson?) that free people should have the right to govern themselves, rather than be ruled by a political class—even a benevolent, well-meaning one.

Unfortunately, liberals have begun to openly question that notion. You hear it subtly in the media's "look at that rabble" reaction to talk radio and tea parties.

At the *New York Times*, the disdain is far more open. David Brooks's fellow *Times* columnist, Thomas Friedman, wrote a 2009 column bemoaning America's messy democratic politics and praising the superior example of China—the one-party, tyrannical, Communist dictatorship of China. He wrote in the *Times*,

> There is only one thing worse than one-party autocracy, and that is one-party democracy, which is what we have in America today.
>
> One-party autocracy certainly has its drawbacks. But when it is led by a reasonably enlightened group of people, as China is today, it can also have great advantages. That one party can just impose the politically difficult but critically important policies needed to move a society forward in the 21st century.

Friedman may have been a bit more explicit than President Obama or Nancy Pelosi, but he expressed what the Obama literati truly believe: that America would be a better place if those of us who aren't in the elite would just sit down and shut up.

Should we accept their premise, Mr. Brooks? Should we just go along quietly and stop resisting this push toward an elitist oligarchy?

With all due respect, Mr. Brooks, we who reject this autocratic, anti-democratic movement are not the villains in this struggle. We are the freedom fighters—the good guys.

How can I say "yes" to politicians who want to strip my freedom away from me? Who want to limit the opportunities my children will have to live a free, prosperous life?

How is it negative for me to say "no" when another incompetent government moron tries to take power from the people and give it to the ever-failing public sector?

The talk radio/tea party/townhall Americans aren't saying "no" to Team Obama's policies out of spite, or merely to sink the USS Progressive. We're screaming "stop the bus" as the dangerous, lumbering Government Express careens out of control through our neighborhoods, our families, and our lives.

"Against?" Were the Minutemen who stood guard in Boston in 1776 merely "against" the British? Or were they fighting *for* a then-unimaginable future of a free nation yet to be born? Were the Abolitionists merely "against" the inhumanity of slavery? Or were they fighting *for* the proposition that all men are created equal, for the inalienable rights of life and liberty?

American Greatness: It Doesn't Change

Some O-bots object to the phrase "take our country back." They hear a subtext about race and privilege, and black folks in the back of the bus. And I suppose you can hear that if you want to. After all, Maureen Dowd hears imaginary things all the time. But if that's truly what you hear, you're not listening.

What an irony to hear supporters of big government, racial quotas, and limited personal freedom accuse tea partiers of wanting to return to the era of Jim Crow. It wasn't the private sector that imposed segregation on black Americans fifty years ago. It was the government. It wasn't free people who mandated segregated water fountains and segregated schools. It was the state.

Notably, the freedom marchers who were attacked in southern streets and faced down snarling dogs were denounced as "mobs" and "radicals" by the government establishment they challenged, too. They wanted to expand individual liberty in the face of collective judgments about which citizens were "good" or "bad."

Reclaiming America's values means defending the notions of individual liberty, opportunity, and accountability that are anathema to this sort of injustice and thuggery. There's a reason that third-world dictators and low-rent tyrants fear any interjection of freedom into their regimes. It's because freedom is a corrosive force. It wears away at centralized stupidity and collective control.

Let an oppressed man have just one freedom—say, the freedom to buy his own bread—and as he stands at the counter deciding between the whole wheat and the pumpernickel, he will wonder why he can't choose his own cheese, too. Then his wine. Then his car, his TV channels, his favorite websites and, inevitably, the future and leadership of his nation.

American democracy endured a dark period from 2006 to 2009. Banks melted down, the stock market crashed, and many began to doubt that free Americans could govern ourselves. Some Americans began to lose faith. But others never did. Were we angry at the mistakes we made as a nation: the bailouts, the bumbling, the politically connected players declared "too big to fail"? Yes.

Could we admit that America and its leaders screwed up? Absolutely—and it didn't matter if you were talking Republicans or Democrats.

Yes, we doubted our leaders, we doubted our political parties, we doubted some of our own decisions and beliefs. But we never doubted our country. We retained an unshakeable faith in the greatness of America, in the exceptionalism of our nation and its values.

Unlike the liberal elites, we don't believe American values are just another way for a nation to be good. We believe America represents the right way for a nation to be great.

After President Obama's election, when the media elites and the president's allies insisted we need to *change* that America—not just its policies but the character of our nation itself—did we say "no?"

No, we said, "Hell, no!"

We said it loudly and clearly and sometimes cleverly and sometimes too harshly, but it was definitely a resounding vote "against."

Because we clung (bitterly, perhaps?) to our vision of the greatness of America. We said "no" to the Obama elites' vision of a diminished, collective, Europeanized America, in order to embrace the eternal values of the America we love.

It's an America full of hope. But it doesn't change.

Yes, it's always evolving, growing, developing—forming a more perfect union, more perfected every day. But it doesn't truly change, not in its essence.

And we stand with it, Mr. Brooks. We stand *for* it. We love it. And we will fight for it to our very last breath.

Because there is really only one thing we are "against."

Quitting.

Tell that to your friends at the *New York Times*, maybe to President Obama, too. And tell them they might as well get used to us.

Because we tea-partying, townhalling, talk-radio-listening, freedom-loving, hell-raising Americans are here to stay.

Acknowledgments

Special thanks to my mother for allowing me to use her as a central character in this story. She has suffered the most painful treatment any person can endure from a writer: accurate reporting. Thank you to Jennifer Hamilton, Amy Kane, Bill Duggan, Jim Fister, Madeline Anderson, Brian Cary, kansasmeadowlark.com, granitegrok.com, and to 96.9 WTKK for the terrific photos that appear in this book of homemade signs from townhalls and tea parties across the country.

Thanks to Jack Langer at Regnery for turning my random nouns and verbs into somewhat coherent sentences; to Julie for her input and (mostly) her patience; to Glenn Beck, Michelle Malkin, and Glenn Reynolds for their essential role in creating the tea party movement; to my 96.9 WTKK listeners for demanding I be a part of it; and to Peter, Tom, Grace, and everyone at Greater Media Boston for letting me jump into the tea party project—and this book—without reservation.

But my greatest, most heartfelt thanks to Mencken, Alexandra, Galen Luke, and Katherine Grace for letting Daddy work when he really needed to—and for letting him play when he needed that, too.

Index